Are You Worthy of Him?

By
Fabian F. Harper

Obedient To The Point Of Death

Library of Congress Control Number:		2018907478
ISBN:	Hardcover	978-1-9845-3696-9
	Softcover	978-1-9845-3697-6
	eBook	978-1-9845-3698-3

Print information available on the last page.

Rev. date: 10/16/2018

To order additional copies of this book, contact:
Xlibris
1-888-795-4274
www.Xlibris.com
Orders@Xlibris.com
780032

Table of Contents

Chapter 3

Chapter 4

Chapter 5

Chapter 6

Chapter 7

Chapter 8

Chapter 9

Chapter 10

Chapter 11

Chapter 12

Note of Thanks

I will like to take this opportunity to graciously extend a sense of gratitude to my editorial support team for their diligence and insightful aid in scrutinizing the content of the text.

Indeed, their persistent and passionate efforts have galvanized my faith while deepening my desire to excel and evolve in the grace of God. Thank you so much and may your diligent service serve to promote future publications that advance the Kingdom of God. Also, I will like to extend a deep sense of gratitude to my elder sister Juliana Harper who has dedicated her tremendous artistic creativity to all my past and now present publications.

Introduction

Are You Worthy of Him?

We are worthy of him when our love for him is both supreme and exclusive. **Worthiness is the relational result of a centralized love objective.** Our love for God must transcend every competing desire that challenges the worthiness of our walk. You cannot be worthy of a King with divided loyalties that compromises his reign in your heart. Worthiness implies that following him is charged to your account and the price is sacrificial and progressively demanding. To endorse the dignity of his reign, the King of Kings must rule from inside out so that the supremacy of his worth is witnessed and glorified among men.

Are You Worthy Of Him?

To walk worthy of him is both costly and rewarding. Anything that undermined or competes with your love for God disqualifies the worthiness of the relationship. God cannot be reduced, replaced or repelled by inferior loyalties that diminish his supremacy in your heart. To be worthy of Him your love objective must be un-contested and paramount. He must be the consuming objective that permits the subjective assurance that qualifies his worth.

This type of love obligation is self-defining, self-revealing and self-sacrificial in content. It is within the rubric of this love engagement that I abandon my life to find its true purpose, worth, and destiny. The true value of my life is unveiled as it is surrendered not kept. Being worthy of the King is conditioned and confirmed in this principle. Your worthiness is evaluated by your surrender to someone greater than yourself. Your self-worth is not exclusively determined by you, but by the God, you surrendered to. Surrendering to the King is poignant because my true life cannot be revealed until I yield myself to the sole owner of all life. Ownership is the culture of being and the process of belonging. Whoever owns you gives you value and dignity that markets the intended purpose of their ownership. If you are bought by the truth you cannot be owned by deception.

Living worthy of the Kingdom dignifies and empowers my life, giving me an elevated context that is superior to worldly cultures, norms, and ideas. Christ rule in my life is superior to all my self-engendered ambitions; aspirations; philosophies, and desires. I cannot live worthy apart from him because my life is Christ and detach from him I can do nothing.

A worthy walk is an ascended walk that models the culture of heaven as we establish his will on the earth. Walking worthy is not just a life, it's a calling a vacation an intimate fellowship of suffering that endorses our entrance into the Kingdom of God.

The cost of this walk impacts your relationship at every level because it presents God individually and collectively, it unites the body by disqualifying competition, strife, self-conceit and all the humanistic tensions that war against the glory and stature of Christ. A worthy walk must bring the church into corporate maturity, destiny, and fulfillment.

As you walk worthy of him you begin to live as him. 'As he is so are we in the world.' Being worthy of him means that I live to present him not myself. I live to present what is greater than self-revealing desires and intentions. In presenting what is greater my life expands in experiences and elevates in faith. Who I am can only be determined by who He is. The substratum of my worthiness is disclosed in his majesty, glory, and power. This is why Christ was given all power and a name that's above every name he lived to present the will of the Father because his Father is greater.

This is in substance why the dignity of our walk in Christ must be honored and established on the earth. We are portraying in majesty the steps and order of an infinite God.

Chapter 1

Are You Worthy of Him?

17

We cannot be seated in heaven
yet live unworthy and
undignified on the earth.

Are You Worthy Of Him?

You can only walk worthy of Christ if his life qualifies your Worth.

Chapter 1

Are You Worthy of Him?

19

The coming of Christ to the world is by far the greatest deposit and intervention into the affairs of humanity. There is nothing that can be compared with the purpose and investment of the Father in giving to us his only Son. Nothing could be more loving, kind and rewarding than the sacrificial service and example of Jesus Christ. He is the best of heaven and the greatest example of God in humanity. He is not just the presentation of truth, but the visible expression of his Fathers message both in person and principle. He is not just the revealer of God but God revealed and Christ in us the hope of glory.

Are You Worthy Of Him?

Christ Jesus by the sacrifice of Himself exhibits the greatest value and honor for human life and dignity. No one is worthy to replace Him or supersede his preeminence; he is the deepest investment, the most promising invitation to virtue and glory, the supreme aspiration and hunger of the nations of the world. He is the sine-qua-non of every heart and culture. He died for you, but can you live deserving of him. To live deserving of him we must invest sacrificially in his redemptive love for us. **To walk in the worthiness of his inevitable grace we must invest in the dignity of his impregnable love.**

We invest in things proportionate to the perceived value it holds. The value we attach to Christ determines our level of investment, commitment, and obedience. The honor we give to his worth is validated through the quality and content of our walk. The very dignity of his worth is then measured against the background of our obedience and faith. Do you deserve him if your life remains in militant opposition to his presentation, promises, and purpose?

We deserve him when we are empowered to experience what he lived by example. A life that is deserving of him suggests that we are indebted to the King and his payment must be forthcoming.

20

Are You Worthy Of Him?

You are worthy of him when your worthiness is appropriated through obedience to his example. God gives us Jesus because he's the complete example of who we are called to be. **When we walk worthy of Him we turn example into experience and experience into exposition and excellence.** A worthy walk is the template of heaven and the anthem of love.

When we live deserving of Him we give back to him the glory he has reproduced in us. A worthy life must be one that is consistent with royal conduct and protocol. This is why the gift of grace is given to the heir of God to reveal the worthiness of their inheritance and the quality of his example.

21

Too many in our churches today have become poor imitations of his worth diminishing the dignity of his sacrifice and the royalty of his grace. We must deserve him not just because of who we are but because of what he has done to restore royalty and dignity to our lives. You cannot walk worthy of him unless your life imitates Him. A worthy walk reveals him not us it's a life that uncovers his incandescent character and regal government. **In principle, God charges us to walk worthy because He is deserving of himself.**

The word worthy in scripture comes from the word 'aksios' which means to weigh in assigning the matching value. It means befitting, congruous or deserving. The word 'aksios' is the root word of the English term 'axis' which refers to balance-scale.

We Are Worthy of His Sacrifice

22

What he deserves draws us into an agreement with who he is, only to disclose of who we are. When Christ becomes your life the worth of your walk reveals the dignity of your position in heavenly places. **We cannot be seated in heaven yet live unworthy and undignified on the earth.** What we demonstrate on the earth must confirm our royal posture and position in heavenly places. **Where we set our minds seeds the worthiness of our souls.**

The worthiness of your walk and message are indicative of the honor attributed to Kings. This is why Jesus told his disciples to shake the dust off their feet when they entered places that resist the worthiness of the Kings message. The gravity and essence of your walk must honor the sacrifice of the cross and its redemptive intentions. This is why you cannot be worthy of him unless you pick up your cross and follow him daily. Matt 10:38. Your conduct must correspond to the dignity of his calling. When you walk deserving of him many will have to pause and say you have been with Jesus because the worth of Christ is not just given by grace through faith it must be pursued and worked out in explicit power and regal splendor.

No one comes into this world deserving or worthy of God. We are all born in sin and shaped in iniquity. We are only worthy because God has chosen to love us and deposit himself in us through the sacrifice of his Son. **There is no one on earth that is worthy by their own righteousness.**

This is why we can do nothing that makes us worthy of God. There is nothing in you that God is indebted to. You cannot perform enough to warrant his approval you can do nothing in this life without utilizing his created resources this is why you came into this world in the red. This is the reason why your lips must persistently reverberate praise and your heart should glisten with adoration and worship.

God is not indebted to us based on our deeds of righteousness neither is he impress by our reputation; social status; wealth or religious contributions. God cannot owe because there is nothing you can have that is not given dependent upon him. 'The earth is still the Lords.' We live worthy of him when our thoughts are governed by his word.

Our worthiness is always contingent upon his worth. **When we walk deserving of him we maximize his character and embody his person.** It is his worthiness that reveals our unworthiness this is why we ought to be humble, obedient and thankful in all things. We must stop pursuing dreams and goals that betray the footprints of his steps. Many in our churches and culture passionately pursue ambitions that war against the predestine plan God has for their lives. Worthiness is the harmony of his heart, the order of his walk and the character of his person.

Worthiness Through Affliction

The steadfastness of your faith in affliction and persecution makes you worthy of the Kingdom. The quality of our faith develops and matures through affliction and testing. You do not enter the Kingdom because of inherent worth or rights you enter because your worth has been tested and approved. It is through many trials we enter the Kingdom of God Act 14:22. God will not trust you where you have not been proven and tested. It is through the test and the proven realities of victory that trust is confirmed and worthiness endorsed.

If your walk is not worthy are you qualified to share his message? *A worthy walk means that the strength of your message must be balanced by the dignity of your character.* This is why your worth must be approved through affliction and persecution. The church can no longer declare a powerful message yet demonstrate a weak character. *The product must be consistent with the dignity of the manufacturer.*

It is through unearned suffering we are commended. When we suffer for what's right it's credited to our account and it receives God's approval. We are called and appointed to suffer for righteousness sake. In the Kingdom, we are commissioned to the unearned suffering that dignifies our redemption. Unjust suffering is God's approval process it's the key to divine favor. What you are willing to suffer for is an index to what you are willing to die too.

26

The effectiveness of your ministry, business or institution must be seen in the worthiness of your walk. To be deserving of him we must be made by his worthiness. You cannot produce what you are not made of. Production is the benefit of assimilation and consumption. This is the same reason why a Great nation cannot consistently produce weak and dysfunctional families. You are what you produce this is the reason why Christ said a tree is known by its fruit. *The tree that bears the most fruit gets pelted with the most stones. Greatness is processed in the laboratory of affliction.* The greatness of a nation is galvanized through its ability to suffer for what's right. Greatness must be seen by how we treat the poor, elderly and those who have sacrifice to defend and enhance our liberties and standards. This criteria for greatness must also be distinguished in ministries both small and large.

In so many ministries today we have created a social market for comfort, enticement, and worldly pollution. We are loyal only to the realities we control. We preach what sells because we worship what's popular, comforting and marketable. We are always careful not to offend because social acceptance carries more gravity and honor than the royal saltiness of the Kingdom. We think that being relevant is more important than being relational and biblically promising. We ride the waves of political expediency to avoid the high tides of offense that may disturb our religious image and popularity. In this process, we gracefully reduce the worthiness of the King by marketing our fears and not our faith in him. In so many ways we have opened the door to perversions that have caused us to develop twisted ways of justifying it with scripture.

We have reduced the worth of the King through an emotional and intellectual message that's detached from the transforming power of his counsel and grace. *So many preachers will confess him when they are trying to sell him like Judas yet others will deny him when they are trying to save*

27

their own skin like Peter. We major in form but minor in substance that substantiates the Kingdom. Must we pause and ask ourselves a bonafide question do we really love Jesus? Are we following Him or what we think about Him? Is it safe to conclude that we have developed a Jesus that's at war with the purpose of Jesus? Can we affirm in all honesty that we have created an unworthiness about Jesus that's keeping people from Jesus. Yes indeed we have marketed a Jesus that's militates against production in God. We have discounted the heavy tariffs heaven has placed on worthiness of his name.

How can we prostitute his purpose and devalue what he endured to purchase our redemption? How can we reduce him to a price devoid of his true worth and honor? It's through affliction that purity and honor are restored giving worth to the vocation of our calling.

Feeling Unworthy

In the seven chapter of Luke a centurion reached out to Christ through deputizing

Feeling Unworthy

Jewish elders and sending them to plead on behalf of his servant. The Centurion servant had an invitation from death through an illness and was getting ready to inaugurate him into the unknown. As Christ was near the home of the Centurion he sent his friends to forbid him from coming under his roof because he felt unworthy both to come to Christ and to have him come under his roof. The Centurion sends his friends as Jesus was nearing the home to compel him to, *'just say the word,'* and his servant will be healed. Notice that this humble man sets the condition for the power of God to be released 'just say the word.' The level of his faith speaks to the level of his humility. Your confidence in God comes out of your humility in God. His humility was erected on the pillars of honor. He trusted the worth of the word above his feelings of unworthiness. What we desire from God must move us beyond the limitations we behold in ourselves. Even when we feel unworthy we must depend on the gravity and worthiness of his word. His worthiness can be trusted to restore confidence and establish consolation.

The humble in spirit will retain honor.
Proverbs 29:23

The Impact of Words

*T*his Centurion didn't reach out to Christ because of who he was, but because of who Christ is eternally. He was able to trust God even when his character was unworthy of him. What he felt about himself did not inhibit what he believed God can do. The centurion never allowed his feelings the ability to compromise his servant healing. He was true to himself yet convince about the authority of Christ power to perform.

30

Is it possible for you to be undeserving of him yet confident of his power to perform? Unfit for his presence yet open to the power and outcome of his words. Never allow what you feel to get in the path of your healing, transformation, and destiny. You can be real about your condition yet open and convince about the impact of His reality and words.

Until you are true to self you can never be real about what God can do. Until I see myself in light of who he is my faith can never be great. The Centurion's faith caused Jesus to testify *"I have not* *found so great faith, no not in Israel."* Jesus had to testify that this man's faith was exclusive and great. This Centurion did not allow unworthy thoughts to pollute the purity of his faith. **Personal assessment must never overshadow divine conviction. What I feel should not dismiss my trust in what God can do.** My feelings must never impede my intercession for my family community or nation. Feelings may be real but it must never pollute or diminish the potency and purpose of God's word. When impure thoughts and feelings become a filter for God's word we distort and misrepresent the integrity of our faith.

31

Notice in this text that Jesus only respond when he saw the centurion faith he was not impressed by his love for the nation or the building of a synagogue for the Jews. Christ did not marvel at the worthiness of his military image, social status, reputation or kindness only his faith made the King marvel.

When you are in touch like this Centurion with your authentic-self, feelings of unworthiness give credence to honor and humility in the Kingdom. It's important to underscore that the centurion did not feel worthy because he built a synagogue or loved the nation of Israel. The Centurion sense of unworthiness was not derived from his social or religious status it came from the honor he attributed to the King of Kings. He felt undeserving in light of the majesty of Jesus worthiness.

Notice he had more esteem for Christ than the religious institutions of his day. His military reputation and humility underscored his profound sense of honor he had for God. He used his military training and experience to devolve reverence for God.

32

Obedience is a discipline that explains the love of God.

Chapter 2

Supreme Love Exclusive Relationship

33

I become what I am when
I love him with all
that I am.

Your need for God must be greater than what you need from God.

Chapter 2

Supreme Love Exclusive Relationship

Our love for God must display in totality the supremacy of his person and the exclusivity of our relationship with him. There is no relationship on earth that exceeds, compels and exacts the same level of dedication, dependence, and commitment. There is nothing that must compete or be compared with our love for God. Anything that competes with our complete, exclusive love for him disqualifies our worthiness of him. Our love for God must serve exclusively as the foundation for every other relationship that impacts the destiny, direction, and development of our lives.

There is no encounter that can disarm the impact and importance of our love for him nothing in the natural or supernatural realm must circumvent the depth, quality, and supremacy of our love for him. We walk worthy when our love for God is manifested in our desires, decisions, and destiny.

And thou shall love the Love thy God with all thy heart, and with all thy soul, and with all thy mind and with all thy strength: this is the first commandment. Mk 12:30

God the Father places a command upon his children that ignores our in-abilities. He calls for us to love him in a way that's complete and exclusive, despite the fact that we are broken, insufficient and damage in so many areas of our being. Why would God command us to love Him in a way that defines him and exposes us?

Can you really love God with the totality that He commands if this love emanates from a damage bruised and imperfect character? Am I qualified to love him exclusively if my walk is unworthy of Him?

Will the failure of my walk misrepresent the presentation of his image? What happens to me experientially if I love Him premised on his command? **When I love God the way he commands my experience with Him becomes my transformation in Him.** Loving Him with all that I am announces who I am in the essence of His Spirit. God demands all that I am because I belong to Him. The command to love Him completely emanates from His right to own us inherently.

The Virtue of Reform

37

When I love Him with all I am he changes me into what I am destined to be. **I become what I am when I love him with all that I am.** The exclusivity of my love for him changes and conform me to his image. When my love for him is without reservation reform is release and realized.

As we survey these words and its meaning it implies that he is asking us to be consumed with him. It seems as if he wants us for himself only and nothing must challenge, interrupt or compete with our obligations to him. We must love nothing or no one the way we love him, not even ourselves. If I love him with my all then my transformation is comprehensive and complete in him.

This love demand is not a temporary reaction but a permanent relational fixture that governs the entirety of our lives. The permanence of this command fills me with him so my capacity reveals his capabilities and glory. All of my reality must be governed and regulated by my love for him. My love for him is my life in Him. It is the driver on the journey of life that takes me through every intersection, lane, turn and stop sign. When love kisses life my worth ricochets with purpose.

My love walk displays my worthiness because it is in obedience to his word. His word is the express image of his character and person it's established in heaven and remains the panacea for earthly ills and conditions.

Love Elevates

When we choose to love God the way he commands it elevates our entire existence. What he commands us to do never reduces but expands, exposes and elevates us. I cannot be who I am until I become what God said. **It is my obedience that reveals my identity because it taps into the very character of his person and the expression of my design.**

I am disfigured by disobedience and undone by my unwillingness to surrender to his will. The further I move away from his love the more meaningless, empty and aimless I become. I can only be elevated when I submit to the superior command that governs eternity. Love must command, rule, order and established you in the worthiness of God. There is nothing in life that is higher or deeper than the love of God. There is nothing more captivating, transformational and mysterious than the love of God.

39

We will never rise above contested obstacles until our love walk elevates and expands our vision and faith. When we refuse to love we betray our true image and relinquish our worthiness to him. **We walk worthy as we live elevated by the dignity of God's love.**

Love reveals our fellowship with truth and compounds our thirst for liberty. What the world needs is not another great sermon; miracle or song as necessary as this might be. What the world needs is a true expression and encounter with the amazing love of God. This is what is lost in so many churches and institutions in this nation.

So many of us desire to be loved but we despise the truth that accompanies love. We seem to want a love we can manipulate so that its demands are offset by our inability to agree with the reality of its nature. **The love of God cannot be received minus the nature of its impact.** If you try to control the nature of love you would pollute the intrinsic essence of its nature. The substance of love cannot be redefined or denied by the subjectivity of our encounter.

A nation that denies the truth is in love with its own destruction. We must love the truth even when its demand crushes our pride and shatters our

40

pervasive hypocrisy. We must love it until we are purged by the discomforts it brings and progressively pruned by the liberty it extols. We cannot love the truth yet remain unchanged by its demands. This is what we see so often in our religious culture a love for our version of the truth that's devoid of practicality and power. We see this persistent hunger for a form that alienates power and majestic security of peace and presence.

If we must elevate it must be conditioned and determined by our love for truth as it is revealed in the person of Christ. We cannot elevate by redefining him to justify contemporary norms that appeal to our damnation. We can only elevate as we evaluate the cost of following and the value of our relationship with him. So often what we need is in conflict with the sacrifices we are willing to make.

41

It seems as if we are looking for reward in the absence of diligent and sacrificial seeking. **We cannot walk worthy without living sacrificially.** Salvation is free but working it out is costly and not cosmetic. **Too many of us desire God in ways in which he is not available.** Too often we desire the things of God in ways that dishonor its worth. God is not available in ways that dishonor his credibility and essence. *So many of us have allowed the benefits of obedience to draw us away from the very purpose of obedience.* We must never honor results above the love relationship.

There are so many in the church culture that is famous because they have progressively moved away from the truth exposing who they really love. We can never love God with all our heart, mind, soul and strength yet seek notoriety and acceptance in a world that departs from the truth. *You cannot love God by seeking greatness from a world that resists God.* If you are not crucified unto this world you will be condemned with it.

42

The world can only love and be loyal to its own. *The world is in love with those it seeks to destroy.* When I say the world I am referring to the values, precepts, systems, and ideology that are repugnant to the rule of God and the government of Christ. This is the world we are admonished to overcome and resist if we love this world the love of the Father is not in us. The love of God and the world cannot co-exist as systems of agreement.

The love of the world corrupts because it is rooted in lust and emptiness. It elevates the purpose of deception by transmitting a disguise that blinds you to the finality of its destruction.

It gives a distorted freedom that is devoid of a righteous end, the love of God elevates sustains and fortifies us progressively as we experience its transformative cycles.

The love of God elevates us above the world because it's superior to earthly affections and attachments. Loves elevate it endures and empower us providing a resolve responsive to every ill. Some of our churches have lost the sincerity, purity, and authenticity of God's love.

Exclusive Love

43

Our relationship with God demands only what God can provide. Whenever God makes a demand it can only be fulfilled by him. You and I can never satisfy God even on our best days with our greatest efforts. God is pleased only with that which is consistent with his character.

Our relationship with him must reveal him not us. If he's not presented we are not defined. It's who we present that determines what others receive and define. You cannot define or know yourself apart from him. The only being that can know himself independent of everyone is God. *God lives in a non-contingent reality because he is the foundation of himself.*

If you define yourself apart from him, you misrepresent both him and yourself. God made us presenting himself while representing you. This is why obedience is so important it's the submissive response of faith. He made us in his image and likeness simply because he wanted to present himself in and through us.

44

We are a presentation of him as we conform to his transforming power; yet many in Christendom by representing themselves, unwittingly deny him. This is why God is so elusive and dismissive in the culture, people are looking for God, but he's concealed when we present ourselves. People are searching for God, but they keep seeing the church performing and conforming to what's a common distortion of his person. If our love for God is not exclusive our conduct will remain inclusive, common and unsalted. This is why in some instances God may have to protect the world from the absence of flavor in his body.

This is one of the reasons why Jesus said I

only do what I see my Father doing and apart from him I can do nothing. The perfect man came presenting God not himself.

> **'Then Jesus answered and said to them, 'Most assuredly, I say to you, the Son can do nothing of himself but what he sees the Father do: for whatever He does the Son also does in like manner.' John 5:19**

Jesus surrenders himself completely to his Father this is where his sight originated, in the demonstrating of his will.

Elements of Servanthood

1. Surrender: This speaks to the yielding of ownership rights. Nothing he did emanate from self. *What we do must begin with God.* If we begin with God self is dethroned in my walk with God. *When we become selfless our eyes are now open to the*

activities of the Father. Surrender must precede sight in order for service to be demonstrated. When the desires of God become our delight agreement is evident. Surrendering to God is the bridge to an agreement among men. The deeper our surrender to God the greater our agreement with God and with each other. ***Agreement is to unity what surrender is to service.*** I have lived this reality both in my life and in ministry where people agree with God there's power, passion and unlimited possibilities. Agreement legitimizes the impossible it taps into a realm that cannot be measured but reveal in excellence and power.

2. Sight: What we see the Father do impact our service to him. Sight precedes service. ***Your sense of surrender opens your heart to both see and serve.*** Sight, therefore, comes not through self-centeredness but through humility and surrender. It is said that 83% of human learning occurs visually the other 17% through other senses. The retention of information is six times greater with sight as opposed to hearing. ***Job 42:5 I have heard of thee by the hearing of the ear: but now mine eye seeth thee.*** You can be blinded by self if your focus is self. Faith comes alive when we see through the eyes of the spirit what the Holy Spirit has revealed. Sight fortifies faith through understanding that is given by the Holy Spirit.

Jesus is always doing what he sees the Father do. **Sight ignites manifestation. The face of Jesus is the decisions of his Father.** The face of a son is the decisions of his father. This is why Jesus said to Thomas when you see me you see my Father. The real question for Thomas is what were you looking at that cause you to miss who the Father is. **What we see is an offspring of our focus that consolidates behavior.**

What we see determines our thoughts and thoughts impact emotions and behavior. Faith comes by hearing but one of the purposes of hearing is to form images so sight is initiated. Jesus is the word the image of the invisible God when we receive the word the image is release causing us to see while constructing the very nature of God in us. The word creates an image then image determines perception, thought and action.

Maybe this is the reason why so many kids are rebellious today it is because of what they see their parent's doing. What does your son see you doing that he's now doing in like manner? **Your son is being reproduced by what he sees.** Your son can do nothing of himself but what he sees his parents

47

doing. **A nation is defined by its parents.** We are all defined and design by what we see our parents doing. Children are the functional demonstration of what they see their parents doing. What they see forms images that will either brighten or darken their conduct. Parents in this context can be seen as anyone that's birthing your kids by the visible inscription of their actions on the canvass of their delicate minds. Parents can be the misfiring of a child's destiny. The power of Jesus to change the world is seen in the activities of His Father. The impact of Christ on the world is conditioned and concentrated in the activities of His Father. Our sons and daughters are a graphic insignia of what they see their parents doing. **Parenting is the industry of the family that determines the business of kids.**

48

Children will abort what they hear by becoming pregnant with what they see. What are you doing that you wish your son or daughter didn't see. Your children may have an image of themselves that they need to abort or miscarry if it comes to full term it seeds another generation of misfits and delinquency. **What is not planted by example will be miscarried by hearing.** This is the issue some people have with the church they hear a lot about God but they don't see examples and manifestation that draw them to God. They hear a lot of messages but what's heard does not prepare them for a transformative encounter with God. What's heard must transfix and transfigure our persona so that the world may see the activities of our Father in his demonstration of power and glory.

The real challenge for all of us is not the devil or the pollution and seduction of this world but obeying God by reproducing him in the earth. This reproduction begins with confessing him through example so he reproduces in you an experience before men. It is in your confession of him his life is release with glory and power. Your confession is a manifestation of your faith in him. Your confession is your life-affirming who owns you. Confession is the receipt declaring to the world that the one who reconciled you redeemed you! It is not just lip-service but a demonstration of Christ in conduct and character that causes the world to see your good works and glorify the Father.

You are formed by what you hear but you can only reproduce what you see. Parents may hide from their neighbors until they meet their children. Parents can be introduced by the conduct of their children. **It is what we see that parents us. Children can do nothing until they see their parents.**

Are You Worthy Of Him?

Only a healthy nation can truly parent the world.
This is the reason why when God called Abraham to birth nations he first knew him and was assured that his home came under the command and ways of God. One of the central purposes of parenting is to keep as a mirror before your children the ways of the Lord. You can only parent out of the instructional paradigm of who is fathering you.

Seeing that Abraham shall surely become a great and mighty nation and all the nations of the earth shall be blessed in him? For I know him, that he will command his children and his household after him, and they shall keep the way of the Lord, to do justice and judge that the Lord may bring upon Abraham that which he hath spoken of him. Genesis: 18-18-19.

What we do models who our parents are.
We commit to behaviors that are commensurate with the image of our parents. This is why Jesus never stopped looking at His Father. He reproduced on earth what he visualized in the realms of heaven. He kept his gaze on the reality of his Father that revealed the purpose and intentions of the Son. This underscores why Jesus told Phillip "He that hath

seen me hath seen the Father." The life of the Son is in the substance of the Father. We are here on earth to make our parent known we must never be seen apart from them. *The cattle is only as healthy as the pasture in which it was raised.*

Your salvation is a parental agreement. *Jesus died fulfilling a commitment to his Father's will so that you might live, understanding the passions of his Father's heart.* Salvation is really about the heart of a Father; the heart of a parent is seen in the salvation of their children. No Father will truly desire the damnation of their children. This is why God so love the world that he gave what was in his bosom for its redemption. The heart of fathers is seen in the service and sacrifice of sons and daughters of his Kingdom. Christ did not die to ratify orphanhood but to infuse the legacy of majestic parenting.

3. Service: Is an expression of what the Father does through surrender and sight. *The Father is in revelation what the Son is in the demonstration.* He does nothing apart from the exclusive love for his Father. Everything is done with the Father's consent and in conjunction with him. Self-determination has no place in the life of Jesus and it should have no place in the life of believers. In the Kingdom, the self is denied and dethroned so that Christ can be authenticated.

God made us for something exclusive and supreme relationally. He desired something that he did not have with the angels, animals, and other aspects of creation. The exclusivity of his love for us is unique if not peculiar. He's always drawing us to himself in ways that are unknown to us. As we trace the life and ways of Christ we see the exclusivity and supremacy of his love for his Father even when the Father chooses to bruise him and he agonized in the garden by becoming physically and psychologically unfixed yet he still agreed and surrendered to his Father's will. He surrendered to what was greater than himself by deciding to do what troubled his humanity. **Agreement is evident when self is subdued.**

So many sons and daughters in ministry are unwilling to suffer to present their fathers will simply because their love walk is bewitched and cursed by self-centeredness. **What we don't see is that authentic favor comes through long seasons of unjust treatment.** It's unjust treatment that reveals the worthiness of our character and the substance of our royal dignity in God. How we respond to criticism, oppression, and obscurity speaks to the quality and integrity of our love walk.

When we become hypersensitive or easily offended it's tied to pride and selfish-ambitions that stimulate if not diminish our appetite for humility and honor. **What deceit will cover offense will expose.** This highlights the reason why John the Baptist had doubtful visitations about the authenticity of Christ ministry he became offended while in prison and begin to question if not second guess the revelation he endorsed. Offense keeps us defensive, argumentative, critical and angry. The spirit of offense is always baited and nourished by unforgiveness. This is the breathing ground for despair, depression, and discouragement. Unforgiveness is an unwillingness to release what poisons the heart and darkens the soul.

53

Despite his offense Jesus lavish praise on him and on his ministry at the worst time of his life when he was in a dungeon cold, detached and restricted. Christ will protect and promote your ministry when you are at the worst place in your life. He will exalt you when you are at the lowest place and in the most obscure condition. He is working on you even at the most severe testing he is building you through isolation, sunshine, rain, and storms of life. At your worst moments, he is making his greatest impression on your character. At your most severe testing, He is defining your greatest promotion and purpose. God is highlighting your best when you are at your worst. He's reaching out to you at your worst moment at your most deflowered condition his love is ministering in grace and truth deepening your capacity for more of him.

54

Children will abort what they hear by becoming pregnant with what they see.

Chapter 3

Your Calling
is
Worthy

55

A call is a summons to a divine command, it is the designation of a specific office or duty.

Are You Worthy Of Him?

The command to walk worthy is design to point you in the direction of your authentic worth.

Chapter 3

Your Calling is Worthy

We are called to be worthy of God, worthy of the Lord, worthy of the Kingdom and worthy of the calling with which you were called. We are called to walk worthy of the call as we live in meekness, gentleness, longsuffering, unity, tolerance, and love. The gravity of the call must be punctuated by the characteristics of the caller. What constitutes a worthy call is not what you are call to do, but what you are becoming as a result of the calling. You are called because you are chosen in Christ before the foundation of the world. **When you are chosen, you make decisions from the choices of your Father.** You are chosen for his choices and called for his elected purpose in Christ. Your calling is the outward manifestation of his plan and purposes. It is the drumbeat of the Father's heart illustrating power and glory. It is deeper than a career endeavor, more compelling than earthly ambitions and aspirations. Your calling is worthy because the one that called you is worthy. Your calling is the soul's captivation that authenticates the meaning and revelation of your life.

58

The Dignity of Your Call

The calling must be accompanied by a life that supports the worthiness of the call. What we are called to do must dignify the character of his person. What we are called to do must flow out of the virtue of His walk. *A call is a summons to a divine command it is the designation of a specific office or duty.* When you are called there is a response and process that must buttress the conduct of that office or assignment you are called to. A calling must legitimize characteristics that fortify and undergirds the person that's called. When you walk worthy of the call you represent the character of the caller and the purpose of the chosen.

As you walk worthy of that calling in all the qualities that befits that office you bring cohesiveness to the body of believers. This establishes oneness in body and spirit as we are called in one hope of our calling. This is why the Apostle Paul beseech the Ephesians church to walk worthily in the fourth chapter of Ephesians verse one.

In the absence of a worthy work, there's no preserving of unity in the hope of peace. In the presence of unity, there is the bond of peace and the acknowledgment of one God and Father. A worthy calling speaks to the fulfillment and maturity of our faith. Our faith must endorse our calling so that the good pleasure of his will is revealed in power.

We must remember that we are called not by our name, but by his worthy name. James 2:7 said, *Do they not blaspheme that worthy name by which you are called?* This is why the call is worthy it highlights the power and constitution of his royal name. When he calls you his name is at risk. A

59

call puts his name on the production line. His name markets his character and reveals his industry and revenue.

This, in reality, must bring under scrutiny the substance of our response. We must respond to the call in a way that honors his name. Acts 5:41 comes to our aid it said. *"So they departed from the presence of the council rejoicing that they were counted worthy to suffer shame for his name."* His name carries a level of dignity that superior to anything we can endure. Are you willing to avoid shame to pollute his name?

Would you be willing to rejoice seeing that you were counted worthy to suffer for his name? How can you walk worthy of his calling yet deny suffering for his name? A call that is worthy must be authenticated through suffering for his name. His name is above every name. To suffer for his name is noble and sublime. To suffer in his name must reverberate with scandalous joy and unfettered praise. Suffering for his name establishes the called and markets the business of the caller. Suffering brands and electrifies our worthiness in Him. If I have to suffer this is the foundation of my suffering, His name. His name is the habitat of my suffering that elevates my character and dignifies my identity.

The Meaning of a Call

We are shaped by the callings of God before we respond to its obligations. You are shaped by the advancement of time to be known in the sequence of time. You are not a blank slate waiting to be penned but a pre-program book waiting to be studied and appropriated. God said to Jeremiah.

> **"Before I formed thee in the belly I knew thee, and before you came forth out of the womb I sanctified thee, and I ordain thee a prophet to the nations." Jeremiah 1:5**

A calling is a divine draw that summons the heart to its destination and fulfillment. The heart is design for a specific calling that must be answered by a life that's worthy. When a calling is left unanswered we suppress our deepest potential to substitutes that betray identity and purpose.

Are You Worthy Of Him?

A calling is a deep compelling invitation to execute a unique task that God has chosen and assigned to you. You are known and sanctified before you are assigned and sent.

The meaning of a call defines both the caller and the called. What we are called to do is placed within us by the caller then called out as we walk in faith through the intimate guidance of the Spirit of Truth. The meaning of the call is consolidated and fulfilled in the caller's identification and stature. *A call holds the need of others and the desires of the called.* Every call carries within its purpose the desire of others and the dominant passions of the called. When you explore what you are called to do you will engage and embrace the innate ingredients of your heart. The call is a template of how you are design, and what you are made for you must reach for. God will place you within the reach of those you are called to if you will diligently seek him. It's in your seeking you prepare for the purpose of the call. *Preparation is the face of purpose and the character of process. Preparation is purpose in storage and potential on pause.*

2Thess1:11 Therefore we also pray always for you that our God would count you worthy of his calling and

62

fulfilled all the good pleasure of his goodness and walk of faith with power.

Your call is not just about you it is about the one who called you. You may benefit from the call through your obedience, but the fruitfulness is to glorify the caller. The call of God is not relegated to our capacity but his capabilities and counsel. The uniqueness of your call must be understood because no one can fulfill what was selectively intended for you before the foundation of the world. You are not indispensable but your calling cannot be replaced or replicated.

63

This makes it mandatory for us to pursue our calling with diligence to make our election sure. Diligence is needed in order for us to be steady and consistent; this gives confirmation and preparation to our calling. *When God speaks it is a summons to work with diligence.* God cannot speak unless he intends to work on you and through you. Jesus was missing as a child for some days and when he was found he was found working. Sons and daughters are called to work out their father's business enterprise and expertise. Whenever you are missing you must be found doing your Father's business.

Don't Resist Your Calling

When Moses was called he resisted the call by seeking deliverance from his calling he saw himself unfit for the task yet fit to resist and argue with God. Like Jonah he was trying to escape his assignment by talking God out his calling. Moses failed to see that the call of God is the merging of his incapacities with God capabilities.

What qualified him was perceived as a disqualifying factor. He emphatically sold God his vision of himself with the hope that God will renounce His intended vision for his life. A call will expose your insecurities yet draw you to the most secure relational investment. **A call is that magnetic pull through passions that inflame the heart with purposeful delight.**

To resist your call compromises, the very destiny and development of your life. You live every waking moment in conflict and betrayal with your intended purpose, passion and plan. Your calling must be uncovered early so that you develop in proportion to your assign pursuit and passion. So many miss the importance of this early revelation as they journey through the times and seasons of life in a state of wonder and developmental conflict. You must pursue him in relation-ship so that purpose can be reveal and entrusted. As relationship matures, purpose is unveiled in splendor and glory. The context for purposeful commitment and covenant is intimacy with the Father. You cannot know what's in his heart for you until you seek him with all your heart so that callings and assignments are realized. Your call is greater than your talents more elevated than your ambitions it is a subpoena from heaven subsidized by grace and substantiated in love. When you resist the call you may be present but inactivated and unaccounted for in the annals of eternal rewards.

65

You may escape the call of God now, but you will never escape the consequence of resisting the call. I have met literally hundreds of believers who don't know their calling and remain in a state of wonder for most of their life regarding the specifics of their purpose. In some instances, I would advise them to seek God concerning their true identity because identity must precede purpose. Who I am must precede and compliment what I do. This is important because who I am is a revelation of what I do. The poet Hopkins affirms, "What I do is me: for that I came." Who Jesus is remains consistent with what he did on the earth. So many of us see this as important but not important enough to genuinely and purposefully pursue. *A call operationalize who you are by unveiling what you do.*

66

God desires to show us who we are and who we are called to be sometimes through dreams, visions, intuitive promptings reveal by the Spirit of truth and encounters with those he has given a prophetic word for us. It can be revealed as we grow in relationship with him seeking him with all our heart. *It is the search of your heart that uncovers the intentions of his heart's delight for your life.*

Personally I received my calling one day while coming from work on the crowded streets of New York through a word of knowledge from a passionate female preacher. She was anointed, direct and confrontational in posture. Then it was confirmed many times after, through dreams and visions that deepened my understand of the calling and anointing. Now in my more develop years I now sense through the demonstration of God the purpose of his power in my life. God desires to make Himself known through the calling and destiny he entrusted to his children. Now in looking back at the things I truly enjoy and remain passionate about, I can see even more lucidly my master passion as it relates to my purpose and calling. One of my greatest joy remains in bringing a word of trans-formation to the hearts of those that are in their formative years.

I love people tremendously and remain inflamed by the love of God to reform souls. I can recall many years ago when the Lord begun showing me his plan for my life. One night as I went to bed I saw myself preaching and while I was preaching, I saw this tunnel that was turning very quickly. It was a wide tunnel and as it turned people were going into the tunnel, but, as I continued preaching they would come out. The tunnel was taking them into the pit, but the preaching was bringing them out of the pit. This is when I began to comprehend more explicitly my calling in the ministry. It is bringing wisdom and revelation to those in darkness. Not too long ago the Lord came to me it was around 3:00am in the morning I could sense that he was standing at my side and before I knew it he snatch me out of my body and I found myself going at a tremendous speed until I landed in an open field where I saw many, many young people that I so love they were just sitting. Then I heard these words from behind me "Restore Them" then as the Lord was leaving, he said I love you. My heart is designed and defined by my love for them it is so profound that I sometimes have difficulty even putting it into words, it can bring me to tears of overwhelming joy.

The knowledge of what you are called to do remain critical to your decision making as it relates to your personal relationships. Who you marry can impact and offset your calling and purpose in God the friends you associate with can play a major role in your response to the call of God on your life. Associations can both enhance or pollute the call of God on your life it provides the milieu and sensitivity that aids in the germination of purpose and destiny. God will sometimes use peculiar situations and experiences to pull on our heart regarding what he is calling us to do. His aim is to summons and sensitize our hearts in the direction of his will and calling.

Your calling is worthy, engage it, embrace it and explore it in faith. Your calling is deeper than a gift, greater than a talent more noble then a performance it must be known and pursued with unconcealed eagerness. It's an index that heaven has sent you to present something glorious and victorious on the earth. Pursue God passionately He will reward you by unlocking the treasure of your call in glorious liberty and exceptional splendor.

To live outside the perimeter of your calling is to live contrary to the very texture, tone and temperature of your existence. Life can only be explored and developed within the relation-al confines of the life giver. Your calling and purpose must be hued out of this relational foundation so that the worthiness of your walk is sustained by his will and empowered by his grace. The greatness of your life is in the pursuit of the caller, not the cultivation of the call. God is always greater than what he called you to do. What he has called you to do he is doing through you. It is God which is at work in you both to will and to do of his good pleasure.

The call is the awakening of something that would nourish you while you share it with others yet grieve you when it is suppressed in slothfulness, neglect and procrastination. It cannot be buried in the graveyard of ignorance and fear it must be exercise with passion so that men would see your good works and glorify the Father which is in heaven. You are the partaker of a heavenly calling, nothing on the earth can stop you because faithful is he that called you so be diligent and steadfast to make your calling and election sure.

Your calling is calling you, can you hear it's a deep calling from within, leaving you unfixed when ignored. You cannot continue living in denial of the voice of your own heart. It's time to open up and get introduce to your authentic self chosen in him before the foundation of the world. It is the will of God that directs the calling the same will that made you, desires to reveal heaven through you.

70

A calling is a divine draw that summons the heart to its own destination and fulfillment.

A Calling to Fulfill

The worthiness of your call must be seen in the fulfillment of your destiny. In so many instances the initial response to the call may not be an index to the process of the journey. The fulfillment of your destiny is not marked by introductory steps but by the endurance of your faithfulness that is sustained by an obedient trust. How you finish serves as a witness to the process of endurance and the fortitude and depth of your character. It takes character to fulfill a calling. What you might respond to in emotion and uncertainty can only be finalized in character and faithfulness.

The worthiness of your call is measure by the character of your life. There are many of our biblical elders who did not finish well because they walked in opposition to the worthiness of their call. Some started well but got interrupted and corrupted along the way as they excel in power and stature. The call of God cannot be fulfilled in you unless you are obedient even to the point of death. A call of God must be worked out through you but fulfill in agreement with God. God cannot finalize what he did not complete. In reality, this underscores why patience must have its perfect work that you may be complete wanting nothing.

71

God cannot fulfill a call that you are not faithful to. It's your faithfulness that gives character to your walk and worthiness to your calling. You must be faithful to the end to complete what is in God. Your faithfulness is all about your developmental phases in the character of God. Your call is not from God if it is not building character in God. His calling must work out develop-mentally his purpose, plans, and good pleasure. **Where God is taking you is consistent with what he is making you.**

God is working in you to construct himself. He called you to fulfill Him, so as we live in agreement with him we fulfill someone greater than ourselves. We are called to fulfill Him so that our lives will always be pregnant with him. He must be our consumption, content, and constitution. We are made by him and for Him. We cannot define our calling within the rubric of self or timorous ambitions that dismiss the premise of the caller.

This is the issue with some people who assume in darkness that they can produce enough light about themselves through their earthly evaluations. You cannot know your true calling and purpose in the absence of revelation; revelation is given from the Lord who made you for himself. A calling is revealed by his word and directed by his will. You are not the premise of yourself your existence is founded and contingent upon your creator, he must reveal to you your calling, it cannot be self-disclosed or self-discovered only revealed

72

in divine purpose and wisdom.

So many alive in this world and even in the church are darkened in their understanding in this vital area of truth. Who we are can only be disclosed by the one that designs and determined our existence. We must seek him even more aggressively in a relationship so that he can trust us with our calling and purpose.

You are not a blank slate waiting to be penned, but a pre-program book waiting to be studied and appropriated.

73

Are You Worthy Of Him?

Chapter 4

Obedient to The Point of Death

75

The reality of God
is the practice
of obedience.

Are You Worthy Of Him?

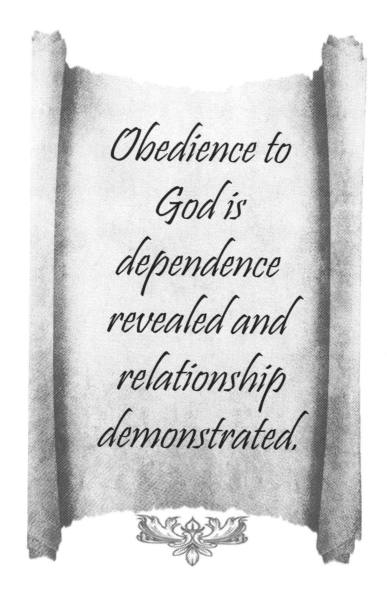

Obedience to God is dependence revealed and relationship demonstrated.

Chapter 4

Obedient to The Point of Death

Christ Jesus was not just obedient; he was obedient even to the point of death the death of the cross. Some of us maybe obedient but to what point, what extreme will you go to in order to please the Father. When your obedience represents personal benefits that betray your love for God have you obeyed to the point of death?

When your obedience does not facilitate your demise nor bring honor to the Kingdom did you sacrificially obeyed God through your love for him? What has your obedience cost you if your life is still self-centered, carnal and rebellious? Jesus obeyed humbling himself sacrificially even to the point of death the death of the cross.

His exaltation was premised upon complete humility which birthed ultimate conquest and reward. **Complete humility is ultimate exaltation.**

Jesus submitted himself to the Father even when the cost was painfully troubling, yet he was exempted from the offense through the spirit of humility. His obedience was so complete that when the prince of this world came he found nothing in Him. He was born for us lived for the Father but died for us. Now he challenges us to be in practice what he has done by example. Obedience to the point of death is a complete life that reveals the glory of the Father.

The body of Christ must be obedient to the point of death so that the head remains distinctly proportionate to the body. **When obedience inspires death to self-life begins.** We must humble ourselves and become obedient to the point of death. This is the mind of Christ and his mind must govern the rule of the body, giving character to sons and daughters glorifying the Father.

The mind of Christ is humble, sacrificial and obedient. In the absence of his mind, your salvation

78

cannot be worked out. The body cannot work out his thoughts if his mind is absent. God cannot work out what he's not in possession of. The mind must possess the body so that his will to do becomes his good pleasure. God wants to work in you but do you have his mind? **You cannot work out his thoughts in the absence of his mindset.**

"Therefore, my beloved as you have always obeyed not as in my presence only but now much more in my absence, work out your own salvation with fear and trembling; for it is God who works in you both to will and to do for his good pleasure." Phil 2:12-13

79

Salvation is personal and individualistic you can only work out what you have been given. God is in you and He is looking for an exit, he wants to work himself out. **The purpose of his entrance is to work out his ownership rights through you. If God cannot get out you are not free to walk out.** Christ is in you and He desires manifestation. This is the desperate cry of the whole creation that's waiting in fervent anticipation for the manifestation of sons.

For the earnest expectation of the creature waits for the manifestation of the sons of God. Rom 8:19

Having One Mind

80

When we have one mind towards God subsequently we will have one mind towards each other. This is the key to unity having a heart towards God that germinates cohesiveness of mind toward each other. Division and vainglory wars against this system of thinking because it is anchored in selfishness and pride.

Humility, sacrifice, and obedience remain the balm for America's social division that inspires her racial disease. The church must establish and demonstrate this solution by embracing the mind of Christ that unifies the body. Without his mind, we can never represent his body nor rule the kingdoms of the earth.

What is the mind of Christ towards the

world and Kingdoms of the earth? It is highlighted in his humility, obedience, and sacrifice which is an exposition of his love. His mind is the character of his being. When we cultivate his mind we become one not because we always agree but because disagreements cannot decentralize the unity of his mind. Having one mind means we can always find a place to absolve and resolve differences that oppose unity.

Having one mind holds majestic keys to the power and reign of his Kingdom. It represents the fullness of his stature and the maturity of his character. Oneness frees the body from instability, immaturity and the deceptions of this world. **Having one mind is the interest of the Son and the revenue of the Father.**

81

One mind keeps us connected through relationship and fellowship. It secures preserves, empowers and posits a life that glorifies the Father through the community. ***Having one mind and being in one accord legitimizes the impossible.***

Let each of you look out not only for his own interest, but also for the interest of others. Phil 2:4

This is the mind of Christ when the interest of others becomes important to each other. So there is this mutual consideration and interest that's portrayed in the mind of Christ. It is devoid of competition, vainglory, strife, and selfishness. Christ obedience to the point of death illustrates this looking also to the interest of others. This is seen as he departs from this world but looks to the interest of others while on the cross reaching out to the thief that was penitent. This is the mind that is so absent in the body of Christ. When the body is not subjected to thoughts of the head his mind is not accounted for. In absence of his mind, the body is displaced and many are deceived about themselves.

82

Obedient to What-Point?

Christ placed such a value on obeying the will of the Father that he was willing to taste death to please him. ***The value you place on God***

will be seen by what you are willing to endure for him. Obedience is by far one of the most important ingredients in our walk and maturity in Christ. It gives us the capacity to live in God's reality. **The reality of God is the practice of obedience.** When obedience becomes your practice God becomes your world and reality. You cannot live in God's reality without the consistent practice of obeying his words. His reality must become your pattern, practice, and purpose. **The reality of the Word is my practicum.**

Obedience is to the future what repentance is to the past. In the absence of obedience, you don't have a future. God holds all your tomorrows and rebellion against him displaces hope and confidence in the future. It's your obedience that releases the power and atmosphere of heaven, obedience is the gate to God's intervention on the earth. It's a place of transit and transition that impacts the world for the glory of God.

83

There are many who affirm obedience but they are not willing to die to self. The fullness of life can only be realized as we obey to the point of death. Most people may be willing to obey but to what point? This is the reason so many will not make it to their promised land they are not willing to obey to the point of death. *Be thou faithful until death and I will give thee a crown of life.* There are so many who are willing to follow as long as they agree with you but authentic submission cannot be undermined by disagreements. You submit because you have the mind of Christ and his mind is not at war with his body. Submission is that willingness to die so that God may live exalted.

Do you follow God because you agree or always understand what he is doing? Do you follow God because his leadership is free of offence? **We must die so that the King can live exalted.** If you are not dying daily, you cannot obey completely. So many leaders obey because it serves their interest. Their obedience is predicated upon a personal agenda that collides with the glory and purpose of the Father. Can you obey if the cost is your life?

The three Hebrew boys were willing to obey God to the point of death; Daniel was willing to obey to the point of death. Job was willing to obey to the point of death, even the apostles were willing to obey to the point of death. Your obedience must fill up the suffering of Christ it must share in his affliction so that we can be in propagation what he is in propitiation.

We cannot draw close to him with our lips if our heart is far from him. Some people are close to God but only with their mouth. **When your words have no corresponding connection to your heart you are absent even while your expression is present.**

How far are you willing to go to obey God? What's the latitude of your obedience? Will you obey to the point of death, even a humiliating death? What joy it gives the Father when we are determined to walk in his will regardless of the outcome. If your obedience is still measure by personal results that offset the sacrifice of self, you are still in rebellion.

85

The process of crucifixion must be complete so that obedience is fulfilled and final. The church cannot be filled with glory until our obedience is complete through death to self. Complete death comes through the endearing love relationship with Christ this is the quintessential verity that quickens the life of God in us bringing glory to his name.

Walking in a Renewed Mind

86

The thoughts of God are design to prove his good, acceptable and perfect will. Our mind must be renewed for this purpose because Christ cannot be proved if our minds are inconsistent with his thoughts. It is within the context of a renewed mind that a new creation is expressed in glory. A renewed mind is not necessarily instant but revolutionary and progressive. The gift of life can only be unfolded through a renewed mind. The outward demonstration takes place through the inner renewal.

When our bodies are presented holy, acceptable and sacrificially to God our minds must be renewed to prove what's good, acceptable and perfect in the will of God. Saving faith must invite living faith producing fruit unto the glory of God. What you are your mind must prove through the renewal process. This is the reason why you must yield yourself as those that are alive from the dead. Your mind must come into conformity to the change that evident in your heart.

God does not work through your availability but through consecrated vessels yielded to him. This is what Christ did he completely surrendered himself to the will of the Father in order to discern his purpose and complete his will. You cannot discern purpose if you rebel against his will.

'We must put on the new man who was created according to God, in true righteousness and holiness.' Eph 4:24

87

You cannot put on the new until you put away the old. Everything starts with a decision which births to thoughts, belief, conduct and reality then, a sense of being. ***We are formed by the habits we practice.*** Internal formation is the fruit of individual decisiveness. This is the reason why doing the Father's will was so important and meaningful to Jesus it impacted and changed the world. The Father's will determine Jesus thoughts. Jesus lived in the Father's world because he chose to present to humanity what was greater than himself. This is why dying to self is so important. ***To appropriate life you must appreciate death.*** If you resist death you discount the potency of your own resurrection. Death is the canvas upon which life is written with the signature of love.

Becoming What You Decide

88 Your world begins with a decision changing your decision can alter your world. Decision is the making up of your mind. Your mind cannot be made up without coming to a decision. **Decision making is a cognitive journey that's finalized in the liberty of choice. It is the arrows of thought released into the prudence of judgment.** Whatever conditions your mind is a product of your thoughts. **The mind of Christ is made by the decisions of His Father.** The birthing of your thoughts must begin in the disposition of your Father. **Decisions are the resting place for your thoughts.** Decisions are acts of closure to both thoughts and emotions.

Decisions initiate a system or process of becoming. **You become what you decide.** This is why God created us with the capacity and capability to choose. Your decisions are the burial ground of your thoughts. Every thought pursued finds its burial in the cemetery of decisiveness, giving birth to the character of your destiny. It's decision that determines direction, development, and destiny.

We were made by choice for choice. You are not a product of your environment but a product of your choices. **It is through the doors of thought you enter the house of decision.** The expression of thought cannot be evident until a decision is made. **Your destiny in God is captured through your decisiveness in Him.**

89

When you decide you cut yourself off from everything else by making a fixed and determined judgment. The people that go to heaven decide to put their trust in God; this is why you will not go to hell by accident or end up in heaven by chance. You will never spend everlasting life in a place against your will. **Your permanent future is determined by your current decisions. Your destiny is defined by your decisions and developed by your disposition. Decision is the face of disposition.** Whatever you decide represents the character of your development and destiny.

Are You Worthy Of Him?

It is the quality of your decisions that impact the constitution of your character. Freedom of choice must be managed by levels of accountability. *You must bear the fruit of your choices in order to confront the heart of your character.* What we are can escape us if we fail to be responsible in facing the product of our choices. We cannot know what we refuse to face.

Some people are in love with a self they avoid, the minute they are confronted resistance and avoidance are expressed through accusation or discounting someone else. Who you are cannot be denied if you are held accountable. This is the premise upon which God entered the garden questioning Adam after they had sinned. He desire that he face himself, but Adam denied his sin by discounting and accusing his wife. Cain then followed the same paradigm when confronted he deflected the view of himself by refusing to absolved his bitterness through submission and repentance.

What we see in ourselves we dismiss through discomfort while accusing others in self-righteousness. The truth exposes but love covers, God will never expose what he cannot cover and transform. It is important that we guard our decisiveness by centering our will in agreement with his ways and word. The most secure place in the world is in the will of God.

> *What God said must create your world, not what you see in the world he created. Whoever controls your world defines your reality.*

92

God supervises the industry of his words when he speaks he releases his power to perform.

Chapter 5

The Worthiness Of His Mind

A mind design for glory
is condition by the end of
a thing.

Are You Worthy Of Him?

The mind of Christ is made by the decisions of his Father.

Chapter 5

The Worthiness of His Mind

The worthiness of his mind expresses the fullness of his person. We are complete in him through the fullness of his character and the worthiness of his person. Christ did not seek to please himself but allowed our reproaches to fall on him. We must be likeminded by being in experience what he was by example. The worthiness of his mind is pursued in service of others as it aids their growth and transformation while glorifying the Father.

In his mind he never used or pursued his happiness as a standard upon which to treat others. His mindset was to bless, serve and glorify the Father. We must be committed on the same level of consciousness as we serve each other. **When we don't serve each other we do a disservice to God by dishonoring the example of his Son.**

For whatever things were writ-ten before were written for our learn-ing, that we through the patience and comfort of scriptures might have hope. Now may the God of pat-ience and comfort grant you to be like-minded toward one an-other, according to Christ Jesus. Romans 15:4-5

96

The patience of scripture comes as we di-gest the word, we become what we assim-ilate. To be mature patience must do its complete work. The patience that inculcates must be exhibited in love. **Patience is grace implanted in the heart through the love of God.** If you live the word, the grace of patience will possess and stabi-lize your walk of faith. Patience brings us to a level of steadiness in the character of God that orients us towards his timing and ways.

It processes into our nature the very charac-ter of God through the substance of his word.

But let patience have its perfect work that you may be perfect and

complete lacking nothing. James 1:4

This is in really the worthiness of his mind disclosed through the patience of scripture.

Whenever you are tempted to be impatient with others just remember the God is patient with you. Impatience is the absence of grace and love it denies the very nature of God. *It's the love of God that rides the steady chariot of patience into the souls of men.*

We imitate and conform to God through the examples of his service to us. What he is to us we are now indebted to be to each other. His mind must always govern the affairs of his body. The mind of Christ is grieved over the disloyalties of the body. This is evident when leaders and others in positions of influence use their strength of his grace to undermine the purpose of his glory.

What he is to us we must demonstrate to each other by reproducing his mind on the earth. God desires to be known through those he has revealed himself to. Knowing him leads to reproducing his ways and character. When he is reproduced the earth is seasoned with his virtue and glory.

97

The comfort of scripture provides us with the security of peace. It gives us an assurance, confidence, and stability in time of testing and opposition. The comfort of scripture comes through the perseverance of suffering. God who is the author of all comforts empowers us with his comfort to comfort others. God's comfort is infinite, unique and inexhaustible. Comfort provides reassurance in suffering and support in affliction. When we are comforted it brings a level of ease that fortifies us in our journey of faith.

A Mind Design for Glory

A mind design for glory holds the end in view by welcoming the process that confirms the end. A glory oriented disposition walks through the corridors of endurance only to behold the finality of its journey. A mind design for the end must be processed and equipped until the birthing of his glory. The true glory of a thing is seldom seen in its initial or rudimentary stages it is demonstrated in

A Mind Design for Glory

splendor in the finality of its process. The King always saves the best wine for last.

When Jesus declared from the cross, "It is
finished," the prince of this world was cast out and
the world was now conquered by his glory. Death
was abolished and immortality and light were giv-
en through the gospel. The end is truly the inception of glory. The end of his life is the glorification
of His Kingdom.

A mind design for glory can nev-
er be conquered because it's a prisoner of
the glorified Christ. The end results of the
Father will is the glorification of Himself
through his Son. *A mind design for glory is
condition by the end of a thing.* One of the
reasons why some church leaders are so dis-em-
powered it's because they are incarcerated by the
instant and benefits of personal success that devoid
of finality and glory.

A mind design for glory is loyal this why I
believe that the Lord is grieved over the disloyalties of his body. Christ came to serve and his body
must be ruled by the commitment of the head. His
mind towards us must initiate a new relationship
with each other within the context of his will. You
become what he is by being in experience what he
has commissioned by example.

A mind design for glory does not speak of itself, Jesus affirmed in John 8:17 'He that speaks of himself seeks his own glory.' In order for the church to be glorified his mind must be dominant so that his rule is demonstrated in strategic power.

The Worthiness of Believing

100

In so many instances in life, we seek God because of conditions and circumstance that trouble or appeal to our sense of need. Sometimes in our desperate search for God, we secure what beneficial and immediate overlooking what's priority and essential to our development. There are so many of us in the church that pursues God for reasons that war against his intended purpose and plan for our lives. In our persistent seeking at times we place what we need above who he is. When our needs become the dominant theme then we are ruled by desires that are placed above the governing influence of his word.

The real issue here is not in the seeking, but the intended purpose that inspires the seeking after him. Seeking after God can be a disguise for self-center endeavors that pollute the purpose of the relationship. There were many in Jesus day that came seeking after him because their stomachs were empty and they were seeking a refill. They were not motivated by his words; miracles or relationship they were inspired by the physical provision that provokes their intentional search.

Desires that place need above relationship will dissolve into the quicksand of emptiness and selfishness. What God desires for you is always above you and beyond what is self-centered and self-preserving. We must pursue him for relational directives that overshadow personal obsessions that eclipse purpose and passion.

101

And when they had found him on the other side of the sea, they said unto him, Rabbi when camest thou hither? Jesus answered them and said, verily verily I say unto you, ye seek me not because ye saw the miracles

but because ye did eat of the loaves and were filled. John 6:25-26

Jesus had a sharp sense of discernment regarding their purported need. He knows why you go to church and sees the intended disguise of the heart. Truth will always uncover the intended motives of the heart. **You cannot seek the truth and not be revealed by it.** In other word's you cannot pursue light and not be exposed by the encounter. **Jesus is the light he is not a version of the light or prospective light; he is the light in its essence.** When we come to him we must come willing to be undressed by the truth yet covered by his grace.

102

We must never seek physical fulfillment at the expense of spiritual need. We must believe God in ways that are worthy setting priorities that undergird his terms and conditions for a relationship. The worthiness of believing has to do with centralizing your belief as the motive, intention, and inspiration for conduct and character. Our labor in God must reflect and portray the same incentive. This is why when Jesus was asked, *"What shall we do, that we might work the works of God? Jesus answered and said unto them,'*

'This is the work of God that ye believe on him whom he hath sent.'
John 6:29

Belief The Parent of Works

The worth of belief is seen in the confident trust imparted through surrender and dependence. The work of God begins with belief. Therefore, your belief must determine your behavior. **Belief is the productive parent of all the works of God.** Behavior is the fruit of belief. **Belief is not a substitute for works but the foundation of it. Without belief, works are a mockery. Belief is the gate a point of transition that permits the work of heaven on earth.**

Some people will give their gift to the church but their heart is not surrendered or given to God. *They will offer their gift for money while their heart is surrendered to the world.* Belief means I have made a moral concession to the will and authority of God. *This is why motive is more valued than behavior. Character is deeper than conduct while the intention is more compelling than performance.*

God is pleased, not just by what men do, but by who they are. Your sense of doing must proceed from the character of your being. *If your intentions are wrong the command is being disobeyed whether the person is doing it or not.* If your intention is wrong, you are still in rebellion.

Whenever your faith is absent your service is invalid. Religious people will routinely use external performance to disguise or conceal their internal condition. They will scrupulously obey outwardly yet in their heart lies betrayal, treason and the inability to love, surrender and trust. Belief must serve as the cardinal point that keeps us steadfast in times of compromise, comfort, and religious convenience. We must stand on the authority of what parents all our actions and activities in the Kingdom.

If I don't believe, my legs are amputated I have nothing to stand on. To stand in the virtue and dignity of belief makes us worthy citizens and royal ambassadors. This posture today is overwhelmingly absent, particularly among some ministry leaders. When we are challenged by the media we appear amputated giving answers that are politically expedient but not biblically compelling. *Whenever we are pressured by the culture of the world we deny the culture of heaven by representing the character of hell.*

Our belief must be purposefully packaged and marketed with conviction as we witness for Christ to the social cancers of our time. We cannot be socially muted and spiritually amputated as citizens of the Kingdom our allegiance must arm us with holy violence and royal aggression that turns the world upside down.

The Kingdom of heaven suffers violence and the violent take it by force. Matt 11:12

We can do nothing that's worthy until our heart is in the right place. When our heart is right we can withstand the social pressures to conform, because we are undergirded by grace born out of belief. ***Belief is a divine act under the influence of grace.*** Belief that is worthy is the threshold of all acceptable obedience, it's the prerequisite to the works of God. Without it, you cannot rest in his finished work that produces the worthiness of his mind. It is through belief God works in and through us to appropriate his will and establish his purposes.

Belief gives us the resistance to stand against the vortex of ideological tsunamis that distorts the truth seen in the word and demonstrated in righteousness. In our churches today we have become so enriched by what's suitable, current and culturally relevant that the light of his word is burning dimly through the bending of truth and leaning unto our own benighted understanding. We must return to that secret place that abiding place that keeps an open heaven over our lives. The abiding place is that portal that sustains the flow of God's presence, power and productivity in our lives. This is activated through obedience, worship, prayer and daily meditation in the word.

Holdfast to Conviction

As a disciple of Christ the cost of following him is demanding, supreme and exclusive. Coming to Christ is not a superficial adventure it can cost you everything. Whatever the sacrifice to the child of God, its nothing compared to the glory that's revealed by God to the saints. When we are fully persuaded in our own minds of who Christ is we are compel to surrender everything so that he can daily construct our lives as we hold fast to conviction. This is why when we come to him we must first consider the cost. The cost of construction is the sacrifice of self. **You have to die to be alive to anything worth living for.** If Christ is not living in and through you then you are not alive. Your life is as strong as your conviction in him. It's in your conviction that you tap into the worthiness of his faculties. What keeps you going after God is your belief in him and as you continue to believe it deepens your sense of being and belonging in the Kingdom.

107

Are You Worthy Of Him?

We hold fast to conviction when we appropriate the cost in our character and conduct. The impetus of our impact in the world is attributed to the manifestation of the cost. This summarizes the worthiness of our lives in him. God desires your heart fully but you must hold fast to conviction to many of us gave in to quickly. You will never reap in due season if you fail to hold on and hold fast. Your season of blessings, deliverance and elevation is trapped in your steadfastness.

108

The health of both your marriage and ministry is confined to your level of endurance. You cannot reap great blessings with surface commitment and cosmetic investments. You must whether the storms and the chilly winds of opposition that buffet against sails of your life. The strength of your conviction is solidified in suffering and refined through persecution. To walk with God you must suffer with him as you live in him. ***You cannot build conviction on what you are going to do only on what Christ has done.*** What Christ has done completes who you are so we are sufficient in him who is the head of all principality and power. Stop trying to be sufficient in your efforts, desires and accomplishments. If Christ is not enough your trust is misplace and your confidence displaced.

The footprints
of success are
rapped up
in
the destiny

109

of repeated

failures.

Are You Worthy Of Him?

Chapter 6

Worthy Decisions

111

You cannot come to
God on your own
terms and conditions.

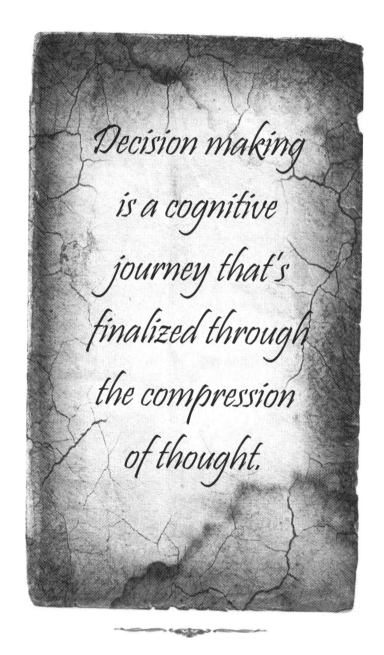

Decision making is a cognitive journey that's finalized through the compression of thought.

Chapter 6

Worthy Decisions

When we decide to follow Christ we are never given the right to follow Him on our own terms. Our decision to follow must meet his requirement as he leads. **You cannot come to God on your own terms and conditions.** Whenever we are called of God the divine draw of God summons us to his terms and conditions legitimizing our claim as followers. This means when God calls he sets the terms and establishes the standards of operation. No one can enter heaven on their own terms this is why you cannot come to God on your own terms. This is the reason why we are in much trouble today we desire to do so much on our own terms.

You simply cannot grow in his character or

113

be transformed by him, without agreeing and submitting to his conditions for relationship and fellowship. There are so many Christians, who called themselves believers, but they have redefined the conditions and terms of Godly relationship for ways and perspectives that are both delusionary and comforting. They have sold their soul on the altar of comfort and compromised, yielding themselves to what is culturally bewitching. We must return in this season to biblical terms and standards that undergird the health and glory of our faith.

114

It is the terms and conditions in following Christ that determine the health and productivity of our relationship with him. In any relationship that must evolve there are terms and conditions that protect, preserve and progressively alter the lives of those in involve. Jesus in the book of Mark 8:34 establishes the requirement for following him as he spoke to his disciples and those who were following him for reasons that were evidently self-centered.

Terms of Following

And when he had called the people unto him with his disciples also, he said unto them, whosoever will come after me, let him deny himself, and take up his cross, and follow me. Mark 8:34

No one can follow or pursue Jesus without surrendering to his prescribed terms and conditions. To come after God is the greatest motivation, the most sacred aspiration. The validity of the chase determines the investment of the pursuer. When you come after Christ you pursue him for his sake this is why self-denial is the initial requirement. When self is denied and the cross is taken following becomes a productive investment. Where you invest your time defines how you exchange your life. How you exit this life is condition and determined by the investment of your time. You will either leave this world with a gain or a lost. God is an authentic businessman that's interested in a profit that comes only through self-denying possibilities.

Are You Worthy Of Him?

This is part of the reason why there are so many debates, distortions, deception and compromising among so many who names the name of Christ. When self is not denied we invent, suppress and read faulty self-absorbed thinking into the terms and conditions that define and determine the character of our growth and the unity of our faith.

In attempting to be culturally relevant some church leaders become relationally distorted and disfigured, parading a defensiveness that undermines the purity of our faith and the standards of biblical conviction. If we decide to follow Christ, the worthiness of our decision must be underscored by his terms and conditions. To follow you must obey. **To obey you must come to terms with the conditions for serving and following.** This agreement that is initiated establishes both a procedure and a process.

The first standard procedure is self-denial. This means that you cannot come after God for your purposes or for self-centered gain. Your motivation for self-denial cannot be self. **Your motivation for self-denial must be centered on God and your love for him. If self is not denied you could become self-centered in yourself denial and self-righteous in your self-sacrifice.** This is why some believers can fast for self-centered reasons and some people can give their lives for self-serving causes that betray the intentions of both truth and love.

There are many who make sacrifices in ministry, they come to church but they never come to God. **There are many who follow Jesus but not for Jesus.** If you decide to follow Jesus, you must deny yourself no one can carry a cross focusing on themselves. Even Jesus had to deny himself before he picked up the cross as he travailed in prayer in the garden of Gethsemane in order to get his will under the prevailing power of his Father's will. We must remember the law of his example by sharing in the nobility of his experiences.

117

The Strength of Your Weaknesses

hrist cannot rule where self is not denied. Whenever we resist the cross self is the obstacle. Self is the obstacle in many marriages, ministries, and relationships. I am a witness that many of the cycles, despairing seasons and emotional turbulence come because self is enthroned and entrenched hindering growth openness and our capacity to see beyond the blindness of our own limitations. Jesus fought this war in the garden and surrender in victory but we must decide in the garden of our heart who must reign or gain supremacy in our lives. We are always greater when we are ruled and governed by what's greater than ourselves.

118

The stronger self-becomes, the less you will desire the cross. The devil will aid in nourishing self because he knows that no one likes to deny their strength. Where you are strong you tend to become more stubborn, self-will, self-limiting and self-righteous. Where you are strong you will become independent, determine and defensive in posture. This is the strength of your sinfulness that must be broken through submission and obedience. It's in your strength you stumble, suffer and fail the most because you are blinded by your own light and empowered by your own weaknesses. **Pride is strength in areas where God is absent it is the strength of your weaknesses.** This is the greatest vehicle for demonic activity and spiritual isolation. **Humility is power where**

where God is present and self is surrendered and empowered.

In many ways, God has taught me self-denial and it seems like I am always learning it afresh as I encounter new dimensions of his love and grace through trying seasons of affliction. The self that is not denied is the self that is not surrendered. **We are ourselves when we cease to be ourselves by representing God as the authentic self.** Self-denial is really about seeing God as the filter for the real you. It is through him we see and embrace who we are in him before the inception of the world. We were never created to define ourselves apart from him, in him we find our world, being and foundational reality. Without Christ human strength can be used in ways that facilitate weaknesses.

To deny yourself means giving up your rights and interest as an act of love and surrender in obeying God. This is one of the keys to unity in the church, home and relationships. **To lose your life for his will means you must seek to please him for his delight.** So he becomes a presentation of who you are which is far greater than your self-absorbed realities of yourself. No one in heaven goes about trying to establish their own goals, rights, and agenda. **To pursue anything apart from God is a rebellion**

against the worth of your redemption and the purpose of your creation. We are all made for his delight and good pleasure.

We Must Decide in God

120

To decide in God is to grapple with the reality of truth revealed in the word. Our desire to decide in God must cause us to acquiesce with the substance of his person and the potency of his purpose. When we decide in God through belief we continue in him by coming into the intimate knowledge of the truth that sets us free in righteousness. One of the severe problems of our times is our beginning to believe is never sustained by continued belief. **Continuity is to character what conformity is to culture. What you continue in you conform to.**

It is our continuation of the word that brings

us into the knowledge of the truth. **Deception arises where truth is interrupted or used deceptively.** Eve consistency in truth was interrupted by deception in the Garden of Eden. When we have interruptions we must repent and go back to the requirements of the word to both purify and process the deception. We must never defend or give credence to the deception that's comforting yet misguided and debilitating. **Truth is the express reality of the Word.** Even when the truth is discomforting causing us to lose face in the public square, friendships and worldly applause we must embrace its loyalty because our freedom is at risk.

121

Truth is existent and established reality that's manifested in God. Our version of the truth is not more important than its meaning to itself. **We cannot keep defining the truth premised upon who we are. We are not freed by our definition of the truth but by its revelation of us.**

> You shall know the truth and the truth shall set you free. John 8:32

If the truth frees you it must reveal you in righteousness. The truth can only reveal what is right. **To many of us want to define the truth but**

we don't want to believe the truth. This is the same issue the religious systems had with Jesus who is the truth. They desire for him to reveal himself yet they refuse to believe him for who he is.

They wanted a truth that is consistent with their perspective, plans, and purposes. Like today we desire truth that can be contained regulated and manipulated by us. We don't want to accept the truth by its nature and the demands of its value upon our life. We want a relative truth that's deprived of its intrinsic dignity and design that facilitates debauchery and independence.

Our freedoms are grievously at risk in America because we keep trying to define ourselves not by the standard of truth and righteousness but by our polluted definition of ourselves. The church can no longer be fearfully muted by perverted agendas that hijack the family and the morality of this nation. We must stand up, stand out and speak out in the name that's superior to every name.

122

Knowing the Truth

*T*here is a call back to the social order of God revealed in his word. ***You cannot be liberated with a false relationship to the truth.*** Freedom comes when you are governed by the word that reveals truth in righteousness. The word is revealed truth that must be rightly divided. ***The word is progressively revealed in divisions of truth that is sequential.***

2Tim 2:15: Study to show thyself approved unto God, a workman that need not be ashamed, rightly dividing the word of truth.

If you continue in my word, then are you my disciples indeed and you shall know the truth, and the truth shall make you free. John 8:31-32

There are no contradictions in truth only progressive elements that define its enduring and complete reality. To know the truth you must continue in the word. What you continue in you conform to. Continuation in the word opens the doors of liberty. What you continue in conditions and consumes your thinking. Continuity in the word brings security to my character in God. Freedom is only secure as truth continues.

Your life cannot be contain or detain by deception if you continue in the truth. When we continue in truth we enter a reality that has no beginning or end.

When you continue in truth your life becomes:

A. Productive

B. Preserving

C. Prevailing

D. Purposeful

E. Persistent

F. Promising

G. Pre-destine

This is an eternal realism that cannot be stopped and it is the nucleus of our hope and righteousness. To continue means to proceed in right standing with or without interruptions.

Righteousness is the offspring of truth and the source of our liberty. A nation like an individual cannot be free or representative of the truth if the word of truth is not honored.

Righteousness still exalts a nation. Righteousness must do the exalting not a corrupt and immoral culture. **Freedom must be governed and regulated by the structural requirements of truth and righteousness.**

To know the truth frees us in thought and in walk. **Truth is an enduring reality that cannot be altered or defeated.** To work against the truth in any nation is foolish, empty and self-defeating. We must decide in God for the advancement and propagation of liberty around the world.

Truth is the permanence

of reality

that rejoices in love.

The true worth
of your life
can only
be measured
by eternal
estimates.

126

Chapter 7

The Cost of Your Worth

 127

God look at you and realize he could not purchase you with anything less than who he is, so he bought you with himself.

Are You Worthy Of Him?

To buy someone with your life means that the value of what's purchased is equal to the price paid. Christ is your life.

Chapter 7

The Cost of Your Worth

129

To walk worthy is the challenge and the pursuit of every authentic believer. A walk is determined by steps that culminate into a culture that crystallized character. It is a life experience that is enriched and enhances by the example of Christ love.

To walk worthy is the conviction and the commitment of every chosen believer. To walk worthy is a progressive journey of change and challenges that produces purpose and passion. It is a life experience that is enriched and enhances by the example of Christ love. ***The real problem in the church is when those who are redeemed try to imitate those who don't know their worth. A Lost***

person has worth but it is not known until they accept the price paid for them. You can only walk worthy of him if you accept the price that has been paid. If you are lost there is nothing in this world that can adequately reveal your worth but Jesus. You will never know your worth until you have an encounter with the truth. It takes truth to disclose the dignity of your worth and the inherent meaning of your value as a human being. If you are lost you tend to live unwarranted and unwittingly disconnected from your true worth. Lost people can find everything else but the true worth of themselves.

130

When you are lost it is because you are lost to your true worth which can only be revealed and established in Jesus Christ. Christ is the perfect template for all humanity. Every lost person is unconsciously in search of their true worth. They are looking for their redeemer subconsciously, sometimes they will sell themselves to a craft, an occupation, a cause or ideology looking for their worth in an attempt to discover their price. They may invest in a movement, a social agenda, a religious persuasion or political cause in search of significance and meaning, but what they are really in search of is their worth. There are times when they will try to fulfill it in a relationship with a significant other only to discover that the arm of flesh is insufficient to meet the deep longing of the soul for God.

Sometimes they will pursue a gifting that serves as a token of esteem paid to their search for meaning and worth. In other instances, they will enjoin themselves to a strict conformity to a specific duty imposed by the mandate of conscience but beneath these ceremonial considerations for meaning is the absence of true worth and intimate belonging. This condition for so many deepens the void and crystallized the frustrations when the real part of their life is not fulfilled or endorsed through a relationship with God.

131

Knowing Your Worth

Worth is not something that is discovered but revealed by the one who is the fountain and substance of your value. The true value, dignity, and meaning of your life are disclosed and progressively revealed through a love encounter and relationship with Christ. His reality can only become yours through obedience that conforms and transforms us into his intended image. **The reality of God is the practicum of obedience.**

Until you obey God you will never come into the reality of who you are and his intended purpose and passion for your existence. It's your obedience that releases the substance and benefits of your true worth and dignity. Obedience gives us permanence in a world that's fleeting and transitory. **When love is constant obedience is punctual.** Obedience is dependence revealed and relationship demonstrated, this is where worth is authenticated and validated. Who Jesus is was revealed by the Father through the mouth of Peter. What the Father reveal became the foundation upon which the Son builds his body. Jesus builds his body base on what the Father said. In other words the life of his followers will be constructed premised on his Father's words. To know your worth your identity must be unveiled by the Father. When your Father establishes who you are then he affirms what you are called to do. This is why everything Jesus did was to get you and I to walk in the revelation of his Father. It's in the Father's revelation we embrace

132

our worth and value in the Kingdom.

One of the greatest desires and hunger of the human heart is the incessant search for meaning that qualifies worth. **You cannot define your life by a cause constricted in time if the worth of your life transcends time.** Your worth can be defined and determined by God who supersedes time by measuring your value by eternal estimates. You were sent in time to make investments outside the limitations of time. Time is never your measurement but your servant submitted to you as you conform to eternal verities. Indeed you are a spiritual being imbued with a flash of divine insignia ingratiated and inscribed through the tentacles of time and season.

You must come to Christ wherever and whoever you are Christ and Christ alone sums up and dignifies your life by giving to you his own. His death demonstrated his love and illustrated the splendor of your worth at the cross. This is the reason why you have been redeemed by royal blood. Give your life today, he is waiting on you in tears with loving eyes that penetrates that void that's in your soul. Today don't wait another second do it now the next second is not promised, allow your use of it to be rewarding. Commit to him now just repeat these words, **'Lord Jesus I have sinned against you and** come short of your glory I believe you die for my sins forgave me and come into my heart as Lord and Savior.' If you repeat these words from your heart you are now saved Christ has entered your heart and you are a new creation in Christ. Now get into a church fellowship where you can learn to walk worthy of him. You are now a new creation with a new identity, purpose, and perspective. Now it's time to construct relationship with him by getting to know who he is and all he has called you to be. You have just made the greatest decision in your life embrace and explore it with all your heart.

134

The Direction of Your Worth

The true measure of your life can only be determined by what cannot be measured which is eternal life. **The command to walk worthy is design to point you in the direction of your true worth.** The greatest disappointment is when the worth that you explored is not discovered in the price you calculated. This is why Jesus asked the question, *'what shall a man give in exchanged for his soul?'* What is the profit when you sell yourself to things that underpay and under-value your true worth?

You cannot walk worthy of Christ if his life disqualifies your worth. **The command to walk worthy must be determined by the worthiness of Christ** You are called to walk worthy because your worth is in the worthiness of Him who redeemed you with his life.

You discover your worth when you received the price and walk out the cost. Eph 4:1

135

The price is his life the cost is your obedience to discipleship. Your entire vacation is to walk out the cost. You simply can't accept the price yet despise the cost. **One of the glaring reasons why some in the church imitate the world it's because they don't know their true worth in God.** When you don't know your worth you will always be reduced to a bargain price that compromises the dignity of your value. **You were bought with a price not purchase with a religious coupon.**

God look at you and realize he could not purchase you with anything less than who he is, so he brought you with Himself. You cannot sell to the world what doesn't belong to you. You have been bought with a price. **Christ purchases you with his life, now walk worthy of it.** This is a command to those who have been blood wash not dry clean or sprinkled in religion. Christ is coming back soon for what he owns. What he paid for must be worthy of Him in demonstration, dignity, and direction. We must be prepared to give him what he paid for anything less dishonors his regal empire.

Holy Prescriptions

To be used by God on any consistent bases requires a level of holiness. God is holy and he does not call us because we are gifted, educated, trained, discipline or religious God calls us to reveal his holiness. This is why we must be purified for purpose and purged for prepared and progressive use. To represent God, we must look like him in conduct and character. **The vessel must honor the**

treasure it represents. We represent because we must imitate what we see our Father doing in the realm of the spirit.

When you are pure you are a greater instrument prepared for the master's use. This is why you must be cleansed of lust, self-interest, self-glory, foolish arguments and speculations. **No one should serve food on a dirty plate.** You must be holy because God is holy why should he use a vessel that dishonors his character. Where there is no holiness there's no purity and power and in the absence of power, there is no conviction that births transformation. There is an urgent need for purity in motive and manifestation this elicits glory and honor. **The practice of holiness is the pursuit of godliness and power.** If you are in a great house, you must honor it with a life that's honorable. We cannot be defined why what we are not. We are called to be holy that's our present operational conduct and future aspiration. We cannot represent God in ways that discount his character and name, this undermines our witness to the world.

There is a holy prescription that serves as a measure of sanctity in our witness. Our witness for God must never distort the image of his name and the substance of his word. We must be holy yet imperfect and penitent in persona. We are call to be holy because we are separate from the system of the world and must serve as the salt of the earth.

How Are You Known & Seen?

We must never be known or seen apart from the will of the Father. Jesus said, *'if you knew me you would have known my Father also.'* God did not create you for you to make yourself known apart from him. Too many of us want to be known apart from God. To be known apart from God is to be unknown to God. The cardinal purpose of being known is to make God known. I surmise that the real question is what do people say about God when they see you? If you were to be charged with being holy would the evidence be conspicuously worthy?

Jesus said he that speaks of himself seeks his own glory. John 7:18

138

How Are You Known & Seen?

The very worth and significance of your notoriety must exhibit the knowledge of God and marketing of his purposes. Whatever your skill, ability or avenue of endeavor it must endorse the pleasure of God. Your greatness must be seen and known within the perimeter of his will. So many today market themselves, using God to disguise self-engender purposes that assault his worthy name. They will present God but imitate Hollywood through the trends and trappings of this dark and wretched world. We are called to be known because we are God's choice, pre-determined in his Son with relationship to the Father.

To be known is to know him and to be seen is to see him. It is the work of God that gives us a platform to be seen and known. This must never be used to proclaim ourselves or to endorse an agenda that militates against the known will and prospects of God.

This is so often the case in some contemporary ministries in America and particularly on television. Too much is seen and known outside the prescribed will of God. God created you so that his divine qualities might be made known through you. The knowledge people have of you must be an invitation to God, not an exposition of what he is not.

Is it possible for people to meet you but never met who you represent on the earth? Is it possible for God to be with you yet people are still asking to see him and know him? If we are in the Father and the Father is in us, why is he not seen and known among the sons of men? When God is in you and you in him we mirror the purpose of eternal love and intimacy.

We are in him as he is in us a vehicle for his word and works. We are one in him sharing the oneness of himself. We are not one because we are the same we are one because he is the same forever.

Jesus said, if you had known me you should have known my Father also: and henceforth you know him, and have seen him. John 14:7

Chapter 8

The Salt Must Leave the Container.

141

What he has attained for us through propitiation we must now expand through propagation to the lost.

Are You Worthy Of Him?

The salt must leave
the container

If you are not drawing

people to Jesus, you

have walked away from

him unaware.

Chapter 8

The Salt Must Leave the Container

143

So many in the Christian faith today have drifted away from the true identity, power and effectiveness of the gospel allowing the cultural pressures of the time to subvert and undermine the spiritual currency and potency of the redeemed. We have been pressured into an unproductive silence that announces the anemic health of our churches.

It is unblessed and pathetic for the salt of the earth to remain trap in the container of silence while a corrosive culture of pervasion masquerades as freedom and equality. Sin at times can be dressed with a legal face because a face depicts the condition of the heart. This is why the salt must leave the container if the salt remains contained by the culture the flavor is forever lost.

The salt cannot be contained because our nation is now experiencing a corrosive deterioration nourished by the invectives of a perverse culture. The container is reducing our saltiness and infringing on our flavor. Our worthiness is rap up in our salt inspired endeavors that minimize the intrusion of values that poisons and bewitch our children destroying their posterity in God. The infernal strategies of the devil have invaded our schools confusing and deconstructing the moral frame of reference our children inherited, giving them a distorted and dysfunctional perspective of the family.

144

We must arm ourselves now with the gospel of the Kingdom like never before. This must be our collective resolve, not a selective option reduced by inactivity and listlessness. We must light the fire of revival through the militancy of persistent prayer and fasting because the weapons of our warfare are not carnal but mighty through God.

What is politically correct cannot replace what's biblically corrective and instructive. We must cease dancing around the pulpit with words that elude confrontation but justify a cowardly disguise of passivity and fear. **What we stand in can at times portray what we stray from.** The safest place for the church is being on the cutting edge of expansion and explosion in a morally offensive world. There is no safety in being contained, contented and compliant. Jesus came not to bring peace but a sword. His nature cannot be contained or controlled what's contained and controlled remains contaminated. We must be loving yet relentless, relational and revolutionary in posture.

It seemed like God must shake the container to get the salt out. What is not poured out will be shaken and overturned in every corner of this nation. How are we to disciple the nations if the salt remains trapped in containers of neutrality, inactivity, denial, and laziness.

145

What is it going to take to get our churches healthy and on fire in a culture that is dying in the ashes of immorality? What will it cost to get the church in a glorious condition? The glory of God is the expression of his splendor and magnificence. It seemed like the average believer doesn't even want to discourse about God far less live for him. I have met many on the streets and in supermarkets who refuse to even dialogue about the effectiveness of their faith. There is no passion or fire in their eyes when they are questioned about the light of the world the Lord of glory.

What is the finality of this great nation if the church is reduced to a social enterprise that reflects the culture but deflects the sanctity of the Kingdom? There is a need for something great overwhelming and profoundly transformative.

146

Unsalted Conditions

What might be the solution to this un-salty parade of flavorless believers can they be salted again through an encounter with God? We must begin in prayer diligent and determined prayer that would shake us yet create the atmosphere for an encounter with the King of glory. A Face to Face encounter is now being experienced by millions around the world. The Face to Face movement is the breeding ground for intimacy with Jesus Christ. This is underscored in John 14:21-23 there are thousands around the world who are witnessing Christ come to them in dreams and many are being saved and transform through these encounters.

Christ is not just coming to them but He is continuing to come, enhancing intimacy and bringing oneness to the body of believers. This is being led by Apostle David E. Taylor a humble and meek servant with a unique ministry that brings deliverance and healing to many cities around this country and now in many other parts of the world. I had the distinct honor to meet with this surrendered servant and his life and ministry has been a tremendous blessing to me, my ministry and family. Face to Face is the resolve to our unsalted condition that militates against the heart of God. We must in this season and hour move away from the self-centeredness that is so pandemic in ministry. We must die to ourselves so that life can be appropriated. Keeping our face in the face of God will station our eyes and salt our character.

There is this un-salty taste to many churches in America that must change if the church must influence the moral temperature of this nation. An un-salty flavorless condition takes away the taste for truth leaving us victims of deception. In so many

147

of my encounters with Christians particularly in Atlanta in the community where I live there is this sense of apathy and lack of intensity regarding their relationship to Christ and their purpose on the earth. It almost seems as if they have lost their love for the Lord and his will for their life. There is this absence of urgency, fire and fervency that nurtures the flow of complacency. There is a comfort that's fatal compounded by an ease that's nocturnally stultifying. Who has bewitched us into this unsalted condition we must arise from the ashes of carnality into Spirit led exploits as we affirm our crucified identity. When we die to self we have a weapon when we resist death Satan is weaponized in all his subtlety.

Who Are You Drawing?

In so many of my encounters with believers, even in places of worship and in areas where

I live and work, there is this sense of disconnection from a real relationship that's purposeful, powerful and fruitful.

Despite all the conferences and religious activity throughout the nation, there is this silent demise and willful disregard concerning the values of Christ, and the purposes of his will. Our desire for social activity in the church has replaced our passion for an intimate encounter that stimulates a vigorous pursuit of the lost. It seems as if the church in America is unaware that the salvation of the lost remains the most urgent matter on the heart of the Father.

149

If we are not drawing people to Christ we have walked away from him unaware. Jesus drew the multitude to himself if we are walking with him we must draw people to him. People are drawn to Jesus not your church edifice or the children's program in your church. So many churchgoers are not prepared or intentional about their witness for Christ because they are not living for him but will confess that they walk with him. How can we keep a faith that we don't share?

Most of us never take the time to witness or share our love walk with the unsaved. When we don't share what we receive we bring dishonor to the one that suffered to bring us to God. **What he has attained for us through propitiation we must now expand through propagation to the lost.** Witnessing must become habitual and intentional if our love walk remains evident of our relational trust. Jesus must become our conversation if he is our life, people will always communicate what they live. Are you living in his word if you refuse to communicate his life? If Christ is your life how can He be exempt from your communication?

150

Communication is the salt of life and the language of love. If Christ rules your heart he should dominate your lips and season your words. Who are you drawing if you have walk away from the one that drew you. To draw others to Christ we must be intimate with him through a worthy walk. If we are not attracted to Him through our love walk, we dismiss our witness and compromise the testimony of his redemptive love. We are challenge and compelled in these last hours before his glorious return to share constantly our faith. We must share this glorious gospel in the supermarkets, gas station, hospitals, restaurants, in our schools, neighborhoods wherever we are. When we share who God is we established what he has done.

There is Salt in Your Testimony

In John 4:39 a Samaritan woman with a dark and inglorious past takes her testimony to her community igniting a believable response that became viral and infectious. This Samaritan woman with a history that was infested with the wreckages of five broken marriages tasted living water from Jesus. Left her pot at Jacob's well and matched with excitement into her community with both salt and light in her testimony and created a hunger that facilitated the detention of Jesus for two days creating a revival in Samaria that was absent in Jerusalem, Galilee and Capernaum.

Please notice with keen interest the contrast between the Samaritans and the Jews. Jesus did no miracles, no signs and wonders or religious questions and debates he just told her about what she did and that was enough to transform and delight her community.

151

Are You Worthy Of Him?

The word of God said, *"And many of the Samaritans of that city believed on him for the saying of the woman, which testified, He told me all that I ever did."* John 4:39 A woman with a past that everybody wanted to forget when back into her community exclaiming, *"He told me all that I ever did."*

Now what she did was not glorious or promising, but she was more excited with who he was as opposed to what she did in her past. This woman did not allow her history the power to distort or obscure her discernment. What may have gotten him stoned in Jerusalem brought salvation and revival in Samaria. Observe it was not a prayer that caused this hunger for Jesus in Samaria it was just the testimony of a notorious woman that incited a response of faith among the people in her community. This woman had no training, teaching or religious instructions her life was so transfixed with one encounter with Jesus that her message transfused her community.

Jesus was loved and accepted by the Samaritans but despised and rejected by many Jews. The ground in Samaria was more fertile than the regions in Jerusalem. One salty testimony can alter the destiny of an entire community. Never discount or dishonor the potency of your testimony. There are a salty relevance and relational transition in your experience and expression of faith. Your testimony carries the gravity and substance of divine life it cannot be overlooked.

Marketing Your Testimony

Testimonies are design to provoke an experience in faith. It creates an atmosphere and hunger to believe God. *People are not satisfied with what is shared until they have an encounter with who you shared.* You can salt your community, work place, family and even your enemies with your testimony. *A shared experience of faith is an invitation to the pathway of transformation.*

When there is an encounter with God that changed your life it also changes your reputation. When the Samaritan woman went back into her community with salt on her lips and living water in her heart her reputation was reformed. This woman was so excited about Jesus that she abandoned her need to fulfill his will in meeting the needs of the people.

She introduced her community to the light despite the darkness of her history. Unlike Nicodemus and many in the church, she was not afraid to declare who Jesus is. This Samaritan woman was engaging, receptive and discerning in public. **Your testimony can alter your reputation and public persona.** Your testimony can overturn your private history and public image.

Paul's encounter with Jesus on the road to Damascus changed his public image giving him a testimony that salted both believers and unbelievers. David had private testimonies that prepared him for public victory and royal compensation.

Your testimony is a proven device that can be used to destroy the works and intimidation of the enemy. God has done so much yet we suppress and advertise so little of his works. **When we share what God has done we invest in what God can do. What God has done for you is not limited to you.** In the absence of deposits of grace through sharing the world cannot draw from the Well of living water. **We testify to ratify his power and glory.** What we experience in faith is selective and reflective, but what we testify of is distributive and disabling to the enemies of our faith. The potency of your testimony releases the glory of God's faithfulness.

A testimony can revolutionize how God is perceived, received and glorified.

'Blessed are they that keep his testimony, and that seek him with a whole heart' Ps 119:2

Your testimony has the power to induce the ambiance of change. We must remember to testify it keeps our faith current and his glory present and proven as we excel in the grace of sharing.

Personally, I can recall in the late eighties as I was preparing to start a new job in New York in a very exclusive Furniture store the trains that morning was running a bit late and they were very crowded. I did not want to be late on my first day of this new job so as the train pulled up packed to capacity I manage to lift the chains that connected the trains and slide through the back door of the train, this was a practice I saw particularly when the trains were overly crowded and it seems as if you were unable to get in, but in doing so I slipped and was falling onto the train tracks when from nowhere a Spanish brother who I believe I saw somewhere before snatch my hands and pulled me from falling on the train tracks this was nothing but the grace and protection of God. God will protect you even when you are in error he is your guide and protection he will not let you fall.

I have had many close calls in the early seasons of my life because I was much more adventurous in my youth but God kept me safe in his arms. Even when most of my neighbors will have their homes broken into while living in Brooklyn New York no one broke into our apartment despite the fact that break-ins were pervasive all around us, we were never perturbed or afraid.

He kept my family while we lived in the most unsafe and unprotected environments in New York. So many late nights after College I had to walk these long blocks vulnerable to the snare of the fowler open to the noisome pestilence that walks in the darkness.

This was my practice for years coming home late at night when the crack addicts were out and robberies were current and inevitable. I can testify my God is a keeper to those that put their trust in him.

'For he shall give his angels charged over thee, to keep thee in all thy ways.' Ps 91:11

He will keep you regardless of the darkness his light will guide, preserve and be a fence around you. So many times he has caused me to escape shootings unscathed even when my vigilance and faithfulness was suspect if not questionable. I have a testimony my God is forever faithful. He is faithful even in the absence of our faith-fullness. There is no one more caring, sensitive and compassionate like Jesus.

157

Opposition is the friend

of purpose

and the servant

of opportunity.

Set your mind

where it

cannot be

measured

or limited.

but revealed.

What you

need is hidden

in you because

Christ is in you.

158

Chapter 9

Tensions Between Identity and Desire

When needs become Lord, you prostitute identity. Identity is the culture of being and product of belonging.

Are You Worthy Of Him?

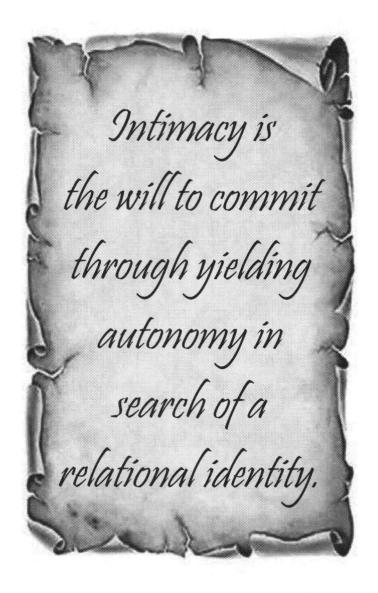

Intimacy is the will to commit through yielding autonomy in search of a relational identity.

Chapter 9

Tensions Between Identity and Desire

It is at your weakest point the devil will lounge his most compelling attack. At your weakest point, you are apt to surrender if not compromise your greatest value. This should not be an opportunity for compromise or weakness but the surfacing of strengths that reflect the power of God. At your weakest point you are at a place of great strength if your confidence is in the Lord. When Jesus was led into the wilderness he was tempted of the devil for forty days and nights after the fast ended he was hungry. Now please be aware that he was tempted throughout the fast, but I believe the intensity of the temptation came as the fasted terminated.

I believe when the fast ended the hunger was extreme so the enemy attacked him with these words *'If thou be the Son of God command these stones to be made bread.'* It must be understood that all throughout his fasting the Lord was tested but I sense it's safe to affirm that at the end we see the enemy most vigorous attacks being imposed on the Son of God. Indeed, I can appreciate if not identify with this experience because I have fasted for 40 days with many attacks throughout the fast but at the end, the attacks became more compelling and concentrated. In the end, it seemed like everything was coming at me the enemy was attacking my mind in the most vicious and oppressive manner. Fasting allows us to gain strength and grace through the enduring of physical weaknesses. It is safe to say that at the end of the fast Jesus physical desires intensified being without food for such an extensive period of time.

What Jesus desired the most physically was now being addressed creating a tension between identity and desire. It must be noted that what may seem like the most treasured possession can be surrendered at a moment of desperate need. This is the reason behind this temptation at the termination of the fast. When needs progressively increase emotions can be overwhelming creating a breach between who we are and what we desire so desperately.

When needs become increasingly desperate you may compromise identity at the expense of need. This is why the Prodigal son almost lost his identity when he began to be in want. He came to his weakest point and would have gladly eaten what the swine ate. Why is this so he came to an emotional extreme so that what he desired became more important than who he was. Your appetite can become so egregiously overwhelming that you would serve it at the expense of your life. *What we want can become bigger than whose we are.* Needs unregulated can encroach upon the equipoise of character.

163

When emotional needs are stretch to extremes insecurities can surface causing us to place survival above synergy with God. These are times when needs come to the forefront while what is right goes into oblivion. The incessant drumbeat of needs can buffet against the character of what's right submerging rectitude of conduct under the shallow waters of desire. Needs that are not detained by discipline and integrity can run the red light of impropriety at the intersection of fulfillment. Needs left untamed can blind and bewitch character.

Job, on the contrary, gives us a sterling example here of retaining his integrity and identity under one of the most provokingly severe testing known in biblical history. He came to his weakest point yet sustained identity above possessions. He knew what he obtained through relationship could never be compromised for the transience of acquisitions. Even when he lost his family he remained faithful to the one who gave him his family. He held on to the substance of his identity in God as opposed to denying or betraying God in the process of losing what can be regained. After Job was compassed and compressed by affliction his worthiness came forth through his integrity.

Desperate Needs

The devil will bring you to the border of your infirmities to rob you of your identity. He will fight wars with you all throughout your ministry then leave the greatest and most severe attack for the end of your ministry. Your greatest battle is coming at the pinnacle of your success. When you think you have reached the height of your personal accomplishments this is your most insecure moment that must be guarded by a humble and childlike dependency on Christ. We must resist the need to own success that wars against our dependency by fortifying a prideful temperament that nourishes insecurities. When we are insecure and without rootedness, needs can overwhelm identity. **When we are insecure what we need can become more important than who we are.**

When self-portrait is weak and distorted needs can displace identity. **What you need can be so strong that you forget who you are.** Desperate needs can encourage you to displace identity and forfeit integrity. Jesus calls a woman a dog but her need was so intense that she accepted it forgetting who she was and faithfully pursued her need for his intervention. When needs are desperate it can become exclusive, compelling and authoritative. Desperate needs can inebriate, blind and numb you to the reality of who you are ordained to be.

When Jesus ended his fast and was tested by the devil he responded from a place of virtue even though he was physically weak he was not spirit-

165

ually deficient. He never allowed his physical condition to determine his spiritual resolve. He never allowed physical deprivation the power to interrupt eternal decisiveness. **He placed his Father's will above his humanity in order to affirm what he lived by.** He placed his will under the rule of God so that what he desired remained managed by the Word of his power. **To keep the devil displaced we must keep the Word in place.**

The juxtaposition of need and identity, am I willing to surrender who I am for what I need? Can desire supersede identity? Can the desperation of what I need become greater than who I serve? Can my needs become so idolized that it rules my identity and poison my relationships? Can I be so enslaved by my need that I dishonor my true liberator?

There are many who break away from the covenant of marriage because what they desired for themselves became more important than the shared identity of the relationship. As opposed to resolving differences that fortify the health and longevity of the covenant they walk away with their desires remaining superlative to the identity of the covenant. In so many instances what is needed individually becomes more significant than the shared gravity and value of the covenant.

Desperate Needs

When your needs become Lord you will prostitute identity. When your needs become Lord, Identity is now on sale. When identity goes on sale there's no profitable return. When we lose our center over ephemeral verities nothing we do can make us whole. **When you lose who you are nothing satisfies until you come to yourself.** Coming to yourself means you must journey through the ghost of false layers and barriers that hinder an encounter with truth. It implies that my arrival at truth is not just about being honest but moving pass my avoidance, fear, denial and deception and coming to a place where I can see and embrace myself. The sufficiency of Christ can keep you in your most desperate need. He can keep you even when the need is not fulfilled and desperation seduces the heart.

He keeps you to bring you to a place of trust and surrender. Christ is your deepest need and your greatest fulfillment. Too many of us in the church are willing to market identity for needs Christ has already fulfilled. *The Lord is still my Shepherd I shall not want.* **What you need is hidden in you because Christ is in you.** Stop trying to gratify a need that's already fulfilled, all you need to do is trust. Trusting Him gives identification to my sense of person-hood taking me beyond historical and intergenerational trauma to a place of healing and reconciliation.

Pride Attacks Humility

168

Listen now to the Luciferian subtlety of the devil, *'If thou be the Son of God command these stones to be made bread.'*
Now observe carefully that the devil does not appeal to the son of the man he challenges the Son of God. He is asking the Son of God to satisfy his need as the son of man. He is asking Jesus to meet his own need independent of the will of the Father. The devil said if you are truly God you should be able to feed yourself as a man. **He attacks the identity of God with the intention of him yielding to his condition as a man.** Never allow the man in you to dethrone the God that's greater than you. Jesus yielded himself to what is greater in order to master himself and displace the temptation through humility.

In reality, the devil attempted to create a schism between need and identity. There is now a struggle between who I am and what I need to satisfy in my hunger. Jesus gives the most glorious and masterful response; Man shall not live by bread alone but by every word that proceeded out of the mouth of God. *If we live by every word we can respond to every need and circumvent every temptation.* Jesus responded as a man to show his dependency on the Father. He responded as a man as an example to us. How do we know he responded as a man, he said, *"man shall not live by bread alone but by every word that proceeds out of the mouth of God."*

169

He was showing us how to conquer the enemy even at our weakest point. He aligned himself with the brotherhood of man without giving any attention to his identity as God. He laid aside deity and responded with the wisdom of a son dependent upon the provisions of a wise and loving Father. Christ answered out of his dependency, our best response in seasons of challenge and contention must flow out of our dependency on God.

The devil will use physical necessities to offset spiritual loyalties. What we need must never violate our loyalty to God. Our loyalty is the breathing ground of our humility in Christ. When pride attacks, humility must answer in grace and wisdom. When pride speaks humility is activated in selflessness. Pride is what we are not, humility is by virtue what we are called to become. Humility is a form of crucifixion that endorses our faith and regulate our love walk. Humility is drive towards God and inspiration to serve even the least of these. **When we are humble we are more:**

1. **Teachable**

2. **Creative**

3. **Gracious**

4. **Objective**

5. **Loyal**

6. **Balance**

7. **Forgiving**

All of these elements are seen in the character of Christ as we imitate him, we manifest these fruits in service to each other as we witness to the world. **Pride is inverse humility that robs against the substance of servant-hood.** If you desire to be great serve. Humility is the heart and signature of great leadership.

Christ Passed Your Test

Pride is that unblessed desire to listen to yourself instead of speaking to yourself in light of what God has said. It is the conversations that evolve out of a self that's not denied or crucified. Pride is the viper that poisons with passion and blinds with deceiving deliberation. It is the essence of sin and the fortress of life independent from God. If you yield to it you are at the mercy of the sinister impressions of your own falsity and failure. Pride is the prison that sentences us all to a life induced by slavery.

Humility therefore is the antidote to the poison of pride that parades in strength while clothe helplessly in the garment mortal weaknesses. It is the humble in heart that's in touch with their true condition and sees the need to depend on the grace of a sovereign God. Humility gives us an honest appraisal of our heart and its tormented invasion by the unseen realm of defiled activity. 'God resist the proud but gives grace to the humble.' James 4:6 It's in your pride you will experience the resistance of what's greater than both you and your pride.

'Humble yourself therefore under the mighty hand of God and he will exalt you in due time.' 1Peter 5:6

Christ is the answer to every test we can take it's an open book test.

Christ Passed Your Test

172

very test in the arena of life must be answered with a relevant word. God has written your exam and passed your test before you took it. The Lord has prepared both you and I for victory in every adversity, temptation and assault. Whenever victory is given it must also be experienced, exposed and enforced with grace. **There is no test you can take in God that Jesus has not already passed.**

The King of Kings has given you the victory because he has passed every test. Christ has given to you the answer to every test it's an open book test. No one should fail an open book exam when the answer is looking you right in the face. If you keep your eyes on Jesus you live face to face with imminent and conspicuous victory. Jesus sat the test for you and as you. This is why the devil hates you because God defeated him giving you the victory, he then commands you to imitate him by living out what is given in grace. This is why we should run to the battle because victory is in every step we take as we confront nefarious and oppositional elements. We no longer fight to win we fight to experience winning, we fight as imitators of an ultimate victory that expresses the posture of triumph.

173

For the believer, a test is not just an examination, but the experience of victory received and enforced.

A test is the taste and testimony of what's received and expressed in Christ.

How can so many of us fail so often with an open book test? Some of us have notes but refuse to take the exams because we refuse to open the book. Every temptation must ignite a relevant word in you. To every satanic scheme of the enemy, the answer is current and relevant in the word of God.

Are You Worthy Of Him?

Why are we so afraid to fight with what's already defeated and destroyed? If victory is given why choose to live in fear and defeat. God has given us something to stand on while the whole world is falling. We must fight, fight with the light of truth and the weapons of righteousness.

We must fight what's declared in darkness with what's written in the light. What's planned in the dark must be exposed and destroyed in the light of his love. When victory is given to us in the light we cannot lose in the dark hours of trials and testing. Victory in God cannot be attained but expressed and explained by our trust in God's worthiness.

174

What Satan Values the Most?

The devil values worship so much that he was willing to give up all the Kingdoms of the world just to be worshipped. He told Jesus all the Kingdoms of the world I will give to you if you will worship me. He wanted God to worship down by worshipping him he would have been elevated above God. *Worship is relegated to God only.* Now notice the audacity of a created being, desiring worship from the creator of heaven and earth. An angel who once worshipped God now wants God to worship him. This is beyond insanity to grapple with the thought of desiring worship from the one to whom it belongs. This is not just dishonoring but satanically rude and intolerable.

The devil desired what was unique and exclusive to God only. *What is uniquely exclusive to God he values the most.* This is why he was willing to give up all the Kingdoms of the world for it. *What is unique to God is uniquely rewarded by God.* Worship is exclusive because it reveals what is supreme in your life. It demonstrates what you honor and love the most. The devil lust after this because he is prideful and centralizes his will in opposition to God. He would have given up the world if he could receive worship from the King that made the world. He thought himself worthy enough to receive worship from the King of Kings. This is pride on steroids this is the ultimate expression of pride in all its devilry.

175

Are You Worthy Of Him?

The world meant nothing to him if he could get God to worship him. He wants worship for the sake of self-exaltation and this is not the purpose of worship among the created. He desired worship from God so he could exalt himself above God and retain what he had given to God. A created being challenging the Supreme Being with what he desires the most, requesting for himself what belongs to God exclusively. He is by nature a thief, a robber, and destroyer. What he desires can only be taken by way of deception this is why we must hide ourselves in the truth of God's word where deceit has no permission or power.

Humility is a militant march
to the gallows
of selflessness
where your obituary
births your fruitfulness.

Chapter 10

The Spirit

of

Excellence

When your spirit is excellent
you are elevated above what's normal
or ordinary.

Are You Worthy Of Him?

When we pursue the Kingdom we are in regal pursuit of excellence. The excellent way is the Kings Way.

Chapter 10

The Spirit of Excellence

The ability to walk in excellence is not a gift but a life-long dedication to perfection in all pursuits of life. The spirit of excellence is a cultivated endeavor built on character development and the wisdom of God. The road to excellence in life covers roughly if not challenging terrain. As children of God, it must become our mandate as imitators of God perfecting his will in the fear of God.

The very value of excellence is seen and proven through determination, discipline, and diligence as we exhibit our love for God in every facet of life. When we are excellent in spirit we operate on a level of blamelessness that makes us shine as lights in the midst of this crooked and perverse system. **Excellence is the passion and pursuit of every King because it is regal in its disposition.** An excellent spirit was both the preference and instructive solution to great Babylon.

In the book of Daniel 6 chapter King Darius was pleased to set over his Kingdom a hundred and twenty princes which should be over the whole Kingdom, and over these three presidents of whom Daniel was first, he was first because he was preferred above the princes and presidents of the Kings hierarchy.

180

Daniel was preferred or chosen because he had an excellent spirit and when you are preferred you are isolated by distinction envied and attacked. **When your spirit is excellent you are elevated above what's normal or ordinary.** Now please understand this is not prideful self-centered elevation but elevation based on the humility of character and depth of conviction. When your spirit is excellence the gravity of your work sets you above mediocrity and mundane limitations. The dignity of excellence is associated with light, understanding, and wisdom and this was displayed throughout the life and profession of Daniel.

It is important that we invest in this vital quality throughout our lives because excellence is the way of kings. An excellent spirit stands out because it is excellent. Everything that is done unto God must be done with excellence because God deserves only the best. We cannot honor him with half-hearted efforts that undervalue his dignity and royalty.

When you have an excellent spirit people who are insecure and fearful will desire to prove you. ***An excellent spirit will expose deficiencies provoking an attack against itself.*** It is important to highlight that elevation and distinction is the breeding ground for contempt and accusation. This is why the princes, counselors, and presidents sought to find a fault against Daniel because he was given an exalted position above the whole realm.

As they searched for error they could find none so they had to invent a law to trap and destroy Daniel. When your spirit is excellent you don't short circuit in your duties and commitments you are efficient and proficient in every task assigned to your hands. What is done in excellence is executed in splendor and glory?

An excellent spirit is the spirit of mastery. This is why no fault was found in him he was a

181

master in all his duties. It must be seen that Daniel was a man of conviction because despite the fact that he knew the law was passed that forbid him to pray to his God he still continued to serve his God. Despite his haters and accusers, his King honored him because he had an excellent spirit. Excellence is not deterred or distracted by law it governs creates law.

Excellence Attracts Power

Power is attracted to excellence because excellence is a regal quality attributed to Kings. This is why when excellence is attacked power is perturbed. The King could find no sleep when Daniel was absent. Daniel embellished the Kingdom with the spirit of excellence. His spirit had an impact on the Kingdom that no one else had. An excellent spirit cannot be contained, suppressed or denied.

Excellence Attracts Power

This is why the King prayed for Daniel deliverance and desire to access Daniel God. The spirit of excellence evangelized the King so much so that he searched for Daniel's deliverance. **When you walk in excellence power will respond.** Companies, corporation, businesses, institutions, and people of influence will be attracted to you in your field of endeavor. Excellence is the appetite of every corporation or institution that desires to elevate to the summit in their field of endeavor.

The spirit of excellence draws promotion because it operates on an optimum level. It is a spirit that beautifies any function it is associated with. It is the spirit of glory. This is why the king could not sleep or eat when Daniel was in the Lion's Den. The King did everything possible to rescue Daniel but he had to honor the decree that was made. The excellence of Daniel spirit made the King fast all night refusing even to hear music that would comfort him.

The absence of Daniel troubled the kingdom and the king was not himself. This is why when excellence is attacked your King will deal with your enemies. When Daniel was coming out his enemies were going in to be conquered by what Daniel overcame by trusting in the Lord. The spirit of excellence is chosen and protected by God. Even the lions were forced to honor the spirit of excellence they shut their mouths in the presence of Daniel.

When you have a spirit of excellence you are faithful, favored, focus, consistent, confident, compelling, organized, oriented, ordered, discipline, diligent, wise, adaptable, purposeful, solution-oriented, gifted, knowledgeable, honored and obedient. The spirit of excellence is a synergy of characteristics that perfects every effort and eventuate every endeavor.

184

Excellence Will Change Laws

As citizens of the Kingdom, we must pursue an excellent spirit in every aspect of our lives. **The dignity of Kings can only be measured by excellence. When we purse the Kingdom we are in**

pursuit of excellence. When we stand for God in the spirit of excellence laws are changed and established based on our convictions. Excellence elevates the culture and the kingdom this is what Daniel did as a captive of Judah.

He caused the King to proclaim his deliverance and market the power of God to all nations throughout the earth.

His spirit elevated the Kingdom and ignited global and national evangelism through laws that were changed and established for the glory of God. One foreigner brought transformation to an entire Kingdom because he refused to compromise his belief in God he stood un-movable and undaunted in the spirit of excellence.

185

We are in desperate need of this in every arena of this nation. We must pursue the more excellent way the spirit of excellence in the spirit of glory. We cannot shine for God until we passionately pursue excellence in every endeavor. We must demand more as we surrender even more deeply to the will and spirit of excellence.

Preferred & Profitable

As King Darius established the internal struc-ture of his Kingdom he placed at the summit of his administrative hierarchy Daniel because an excellent spirit was in him. King Darius had influ-enced through-out the known world yet Daniel a foreigner was preferred. When-ever you are preferred in a Kingdom it's for reasons that are beneficial to the King.

186

Whatever benefits the King impacts the entire Kingdom and his influence in the world. **Whenever excellence is unlocked its influ-ence is unlimited.** The King thought to set Daniel above the entire realm. What is above will always influence or impact what's beneath. **Excellence is the demand of God and the preference of Kings.** If we operate in the spirit excellence we can take communities, counties, and nations around the world.

When you matriculate into the school of ex-cellence you will graduate with surpassing glory. Daniel was preferred because it was more profitable for the Kingdom. Excellence is about a profitable exchange. Please observe that the King place Daniel first so that he may suffer no loss. **Excellence is about returns base on investments, it is about revenue.** Why would the King protect and promote excellence if it did not bring him a profit? Daniel was excellent yes and excellence was an investment that made the Kingdom lucrative. He was preferred as a preventative measure against loses that compromises the economy of the Kingdom.

When you are excellent in any field of endeavor you become profitable and what is profitable is preferred and highly promoted. In addition, King Darius felt the same way Herod felt about John the Baptist, Pilate felt about Jesus they were all convinced that these were men of innocence and would have saved them but their fear of others their image and public reputation permit a compromise with evil. He spoke well of Daniel yet signed his death sentence he acknowledged his God yet it did not influence his heart. **To be weak in a world filled with evil associations is equal to being wicked by accommodation.** Without the courage to do right, we will bargain with what's wrong. The desire to do what's right must influence our resistance and rebuke to the things that bewitch the

187

cause of righteousness. Our feelings can propel us to do what's diplomatically expedient and comforting as opposed to what is morally compelling.

One of the reasons why the King explored ways to rescue Daniel prior to him being thrown to the lions is due to his persuasion of Daniel's faithfulness and loyalty to the Kingdom. The King could not sleep but fasted while Daniel was in the lion's den and as the night past early in the morning he runs in haste to the lion's den and begins to declare to Daniel was your God able to deliver and when Daniel answered the hopes of the King was restored. While Daniel was at peace in the lion's den the king had no peace in the royalty of his palace. Then the King was exceedingly glad and commanded that Daniel is brought up out of the den.

This is the rationale behind the King purging his entire administration when Daniel was delivered from the lion's. The King destroyed all those who conspired to kill Daniel because they were messing with the Kings profitability. Excellence became the fruit of his Kingdom as Daniel was preferred and promoted in royalty.

This is one of the reasons why excellence is a demand of the King, it is more profitable and what

188

is profitable is preferred, promised and promoted. Daniel's excellence infected the entire system and impacted its revenue. Excellence is regal protection against loses. **Excellence is the economy of Kings and the provision of royalty.** Nothing is ever wasted when we are excellence driven and determined. Excellence protects us from investing in what is unprofitable and unwise. It gives us the motivation to utilize our time and resources prudently by maximizing every endeavor to a purposeful and productive end. Excellence is the industry of Kings and the practice of its citizenry. We are excellent because we are ruled by a King and his nobility must be honored in excellence. T**he King is coming for a glorious church that serves in excellent glory.** We are containers of excellence that rule in regal splendor and magnificence.

189

When we operate in excellence nothing is ever wasted because everything is invested with excellence as a means and his glory as a delightful and progressive end. **Excellence is to glory what purity is to love.** Excellence is the thirst of every corporation and the prime intention of every manufacturer.

The King had to clean up the entire administration by destroying his presidents, governors, counselors and their families simply because they desire to kill the spirit of excellence. The King could have just fired them but he wanted them dead because they were a curse to what is profitable. What Daniel represented could not be replaced he was faultless, focus and faithful to duty. The King made certain that no family member connected to his presidents, governors, and counselors will ever raise up to challenge the spirit of excellence that revealed the God of Daniel.

190

After they died then the King changed the law base on Daniel's faithfulness and the delivering power of Daniel's God. The King wrote to all people, nations, and languages that dwell in the earth establishing Daniel's God as a God of signs, wonders, and deliverance. The king began to market the glory of Daniel's God to nations around the world.

Global evangelism began through one man's testimony. One man's conviction purged a Kingdom and transformed nations around the world. **One man's conviction caused Global Empowerment.** On one man's conviction, a decree was created that impacted every dominion in the Kingdom. God does not need a crowd to create reform in the world. An excellent spirit is the spirit of transformation and deliverance. We are in desperate if not urgent need of this spirit in our churches, communities, and nations around the world today. There is a distinct cry for excellence in every system of government but this can only be received through the Spirit of Christ.

The spirit of excellence is the spirit of glory and prosperity. So Daniel prospered in the reign of Darius and Cyrus. **The character of excellence is the cornerstone of greatness.** Excellence is the very virtue of glory. The demand for excellence is the purpose of glory. God wants to unlock the gates of excellence for the intentions of power and glory.

There is a call for excellence in every heart that takes us beyond the cosmetic superficial verities of existence but we cannot function in the extraordinary without being empowered by the God of promise. We are called today to be excellent because excellence reveals a church without spot or wrinkle excellence is the worth of glory. Excellence is him doing exceedingly abundantly above what we asked or think according to the power that works in us. Excellence takes us beyond fear, compromise, and betrayal. Excellence exceeds everything that comes against it, excellence cannot be subdued. When we walk in excellence the prince of this world will find nothing in us.

Then the presidents and princes sought to find occasion against Daniel concerning the kingdom, but they could find none occasion nor fault in him; for as much as he was faithful, neither was there any error or fault found in him. Daniel 6:4

What is at work in us is the potency of excellence that is the treasure that highlights his glory.

The Worth of Excellence

Excellence is the very heritage of every citizen of the Kingdom. It is the way of Kings the very culture and ideology of heaven. It is superior to every earthly system, ideology, thought construct and philosophy. Excellence is an attitude of the heart that infiltrates every system elevating the standards that accommodate mediocrity and limitations. To be worthy of him we must be excellent not just as a state or condition but also as a progressive posture in our developmental phases.

Excellence approximates his worth giving glory his to the stature of his name. Excellence takes us beyond blame leaving us without spot or wrinkle amidst this untoward generation. It frees us from accusation, guilt and condemnation in Christ it is the posture and power of our seated position in Christ. We are excellent because nothing can supersede the potency of Christ he is the very virtue of excellence.

Excellence highlights the magnificent splendor and glory of his name. This is the treasure and worth we have in these earthen vessels. We walk worthy when we model excellence in every facet of our lives. Jesus died to deposit the spirit of excellence into the bloodstream of his body.

193

O Lord our Lord how excellent is thy name in all the earth! Who has set thy glory above the heavens Ps 8:1.

Being made so much better than the angels, as he hath by inheritance obtained a more excellent name than they. Heb 1:4.

Are You Worthy Of Him?

We are in the body of an excellent being and we speak, live and are kept under the authority and rule of his excellent name. We are nothing less than excellent in spirit, word, and deed as his life is lived out in and through us. Excellence is your blood type inscribed in every cell and pervious to every activity. Excellence is the imprimatur of the redeemed and the posture of the Kingdom.

Excellence is to royalty what love is to redemption. When excellence is unlocked its influence is unlimited.

Chapter 11

The Virtues of Being Fall-proof

195

Too many believers are earnest in exhortation but not diligent in example.

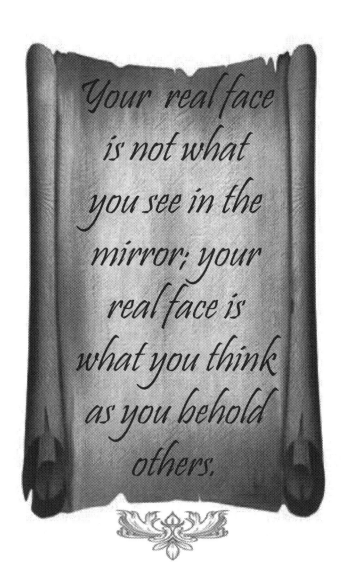

Your real face is not what you see in the mirror; your real face is what you think as you behold others.

Chapter 11

The Virtues of Being Fall-proof

The divine power of God has given to us all things relevant to life and godliness through the knowledge of God who has called us to virtue and glory. It is through the knowledge of Christ that we are called relationally into his character to exhibit his virtues and glory. As we evolved in knowledge through relationship we walk out his nature as it is produced by his precious promises.

When I look at the promises of God I can perceive the content and constitution of God. This is what expresses his nature and character as we received him and live out the reality of his word. His promises build the character of God in us as it is germinated and generated when we give diligence by adding to our faith. In adding to our faith our love walk expands through our knowledge of Christ.

We must never be remiss like the church in Ephesus who left their first love. The love they had at first did not expand it fell. Their love for Christ was absent but their work was present. **Your love for God can fall while your work is still standing.** We can do the work of the ministry without abiding in the love and character of God that gives fruit to our efforts. This is why it is mandatory that we diligently add to our faith these seven articles of grace that floods our character through relationship with Christ. It's through adding that our love walk is galvanized and fortified in practice. Diligent adding brings gravity and worthiness to the disposition of our life in Christ.

> And beside this, giving all diligence, add to your faith virtue; and to virtue knowledge; and to knowledge temperance; and to temperance patience; and to patience godliness; and to godliness

198

brotherly Kindness; and to brotherly charity. 2 Peter 1:5-7

This is what we must add but it takes diligence, persistent work and steady application in order to be fruitful in the knowledge of the Lord Jesus Christ. Diligence in this context means giving haste or being earnest and eager about the development of your faith. Diligence in the Greek is the word 'Spoudazo' which means to be eager, earnest or zealous in concentration and effort. This is your personal responsibility not your Pastor, Prophet or Apostle you must add to your own faith. As you add you build character in relationship with God. You add to your faith because faith ignites and commits God.

Adding diligently simply means practicing these elements of grace that builds faith and character in God. Faith is not just about my confidence in God it's also about my character and destiny in God. When you add to your faith confidence, conviction and character evolves as you mature in the nature of God.

Salvation is premised upon faith because faith is an avenue of trust that releases the power and glory of God. When faith is demonstrated trust is extended and the resources are released to meet needs and accomplish purpose. So our fruitfulness in Christ is established by adding to our faith so faith exist and evolves through additions not subtractions. In essence when faith develops relationship will be fruitful as oppose to being barren or unproductive.

200

The Benefits of Adding

As you add to your faith you sustain identity, discernment and a sense of certainty of your calling and election. If you refuse to add you undermine the consciousness of your own identity. This is one of the reasons why so many believers don't know their true identity they refuse to diligently add to their faith. Peter highlights in this Epistle the consequences of lacking these things. These things refer to the graces that must be practiced and applied to our lives.

But he that lacks these things is blind and cannot see afar off, and had forgotten that he was purged from his old sins.

When you dismiss diligently adding you disconnect from who you are. If you forgot that you were washed, then you may begin to live dirty. If you forgot that you have legs, can you walk? If you forgot that you have hands can it be used? Forgetfulness is disconnection this is why Peter had to remind them as he was about to depart from the earth.

This is repeatedly underscored in the second epistle of Peter the first chapter. This was part of Peter's departing words to the saints as he matured in the will and character of God. He reminded them so that even after he passed on to glory we in this time period would not forget. Diligent adding confirms my identity, calling, election and sight keeping me fall-proof as the Kingdom advances. A Fall-proof character is constructed in the very nature of God's glory and image, but to remain Fall-proof you must practice the verities of grace that keeps you standing. If you forget you displace and discount the elements that perfect your sanctification.

201

Are You Worthy Of Him?

There are somethings you have to forget to stay clean and there are other things you must remember to remain pure.

You cannot walk in the light without diligently adding the graces that gives light. Adding keeps the lights on. When you add to your faith you remain connected to the sanctification process. If you lack these things you compromise the process of sanctification by forgetting that you were washed from your sins, forgetting is denying or neglecting your own purification. When we don't add to our faith we become gullible and unable to watch for our own soul. Diligent adding prohibits stumbling or falling providing an entry into the eternal Kingdom. Diligent adding keeps us from being lukewarm or cold in our relationship with Christ.

When you add everything that's connected to your salvation is affected. You cannot add these elements of grace without developing levels of purity, grace and glory. Adding is dangerous to the Kingdom of darkness because it defies falling or stumbling. Adding builds within the mechanics of your character the knowledge of God that sustains and secures your salvation. What God gives is his promises but what we practice demonstrates and constructs character in God.

The Elements of Being Fall-proof

Wherefore the rather, brethren, give diligence to make your calling and election sure for if you do these things you will never fall. 2 Peter 1:10

When you add to your faith you bring your faith to the highest level of development so that your character becomes fall-proof. **Adding to your faith sustains your standing by making you fall-proof in a fallen world.** It's what you practice that keep you standing in the grace of God. Your practice underscores your sense of surrender and rest. Rest is not the future of the dead but the benefit of the living. As we give diligence to make our calling and election sure we progressively depend and trust. Every act of trust and dependency removes anxiety and fear while enhancing responsibility and reward. Trust is the servant of rest and the result of submission. Being fall-proof is born out of diligence that emanates from intimate prayer and fellowship.

203

Are You Worthy Of Him?

God has already given to you everything that pertains to live and godliness. God never prescribe your fall but has given to your preventative measures of grace that keeps us standing in a fallen system. Grace is design to empower your standing by making you what you are. Paul affirmed that I am what I am by the grace of God. This grace keeps us employed as we add diligently to our faith. It's in the supplementing of our faith as we add to virtue knowledge and to knowledge self-control and to self-control endurance and to endurance, godliness and to godliness brotherly kindness and to brotherly kindness, charity. When these elements exist and multiply in you they make you effective and productive in the Kingdom of God

If these virtues are absent one becomes short sighted having no memory of how he was made clean. What this implies is when these supplementary elements are void in your life you lose connection, continuity and effectiveness in the faith. This is why there is a call to be earnest, diligent to make God's call and choice certain in your life.

Why We Fall?

Why we fall? **We fall when we fail to practice what has been given to keep us standing.** Failing to apply or practice what sustains a progressive walk of faith will invite a fall. Please observe the Apostle Peter who experience falling as a result of his pride and immaturity now he gives us the articles of grace to keep us from falling. A fall comes as we refuse to add progressively to what inspires growth and stability.

205

Peter so humbly instructs the saints by reminding them of the advantages of adding and the blindness and deprivation that accompanies those that lack these things. It may be safe to say that if you are fall-proof through doing these things this implicitly can influence your marriage and every other relationship that's impacted by your faith. What builds your character and faith affects every other component of your life.

Knowledge and application equals fruitfulness. Falling is the consequence of what discounts

God we add to resemble or approximate God. We add because we are all called to both virtue and glory. **If I am not adding diligently what brings light, I am submitting to the darkness.** Diligence is all about being intentional, serious and determined in effort. It's about the economy of time as a precious commodity. You add to enhance knowledge and to create an over-flow in grace that impacts your environment. When the knowledge of God increases through adding, fruitfulness is the result.

206

Falling is not a necessity, but a possibility, if we fail to give diligence to our faith. God never motivates a fall but provides everything we need to keep us from falling. You don't have to fall if you do these things, you make your calling and election sure.

Adding Sustains

Diligent adding makes us intentional and productive in everything we do. Adding makes me fruitful, prosperous and mature. Diligent adding keeps me standing if I cannot fall I don't adding that exhibits my worthiness of him. Adding keeps me expanding and the Kingdom growing. What we add increases our influence in the earth. Adding is not just about production but promotion inspired by promise.

God is concern about increasing in you as you add or support your faith. As we add we create the fullness of the stature of Christ as he stands in us representing himself. Adding keeps us constructing instructionally. It gives us an experiential encounter with our sufficiency in Christ. In adding we inspire agreement in God legitimizing the impossible. Adding is the meat of the body and the nourishment of the soul. Adding to your faith is critical to your growth and maturity because character is much easier kept than recovered. Please notice that adding cannot be done by God it's the responsibility of the believer and the commitment of those who desire to see afar off. Adding aids vision and facilitate conformity to the person of Christ.

Your calling is made or confirm through your eagerness to add giving permanent display to what Christ has done. Adding exemplifies the assurance of salvation it's not the premise of salvation but the diligent working out of its virtue. As salvation is diligently worked out we are sustained and stabilized in the economy of God.

Running from God disables the runner because you are being chased by the one who owns your feet.

Escape is denial on the run and reality in retreat.

208

Chapter 12

Escaping God

Escape does not begin
with our legs
it is a condition of the heart.

*God is inescapable
even while we are in
flight from Him,
His omniscience is
supervising our escape.*

Chapter 12

Escaping God

T he call of God is not always a delight, for some it creates deep seated resistance particularly when it's in conflict with intentions and motivations that betray personal ambitions. So often what God calls us to do runs against the grain and texture of our objectives and desires. No one comes into the call of God feeling qualified or fulfilled some even try desperately to escape the call and assignment simply because it triggers vulnerabilities that undermines confidence in self.

In so many instances the call of God aids in delivering us from ourselves and the centralized insecurities that compounds our failures. Still we persistently seek to escape God even when his plans

211

for our life supersede everything we can do for ourselves.

There are times when escaping the call has much to do with who we are called to. This was the issue with Jonah who invested financially in his own escape. Jonah placed so much value in avoiding God he was willing to invest his own resources to escape God's intentions. In essence he endangered the lives of an entire crew in trying to escape God. If you are called to do something specific for God you could be endangering yourself and others if escape is part of your major persuasion.

212

When escape becomes the determination and not the call, we may invest in flight at the expense of our very life. When we are called of God we must respond in faith even if the call is to preach to our enemies. Indeed, we are not called to agree or determine the out-come of God's assignment. We are all called simply to obey without trying to sabotage the outcome.

Concealed Healings

Jonah's true assignment was to preach repentance to his enemies. There are times when God will conceal your healing in your assignment to your enemies. When you fail to address the conditions of your heart God will expose your true enemy through a selected assignment that contains your healing. In other words, God will put you to work in the area that you struggle with the most. **Your assignment is the solution to both you and your enemies.**

213

Jonah was called to preach repentance without a heart of repentance. His heart was in conflict with his assignment. Jonah desire for judgment among the Assyrian people was undermined by God's abundant mercies toward them. This was the rationale behind his escape but his escape was contained by God.

God used both the elements and the Whale to regulate Jonah's escape. When we try to escape God he will use circumstances, conditions, and people to orchestrate his plans and promote his purposes. Both the Whale and the elements were employed by God to contain his escape and negotiate his arrival to Nineveh.

So many times in my life God shut down my plans, closed doors and disappointed my objectives to keep me for his appointed time and season. He used failures repeatedly to turn me in the direction of his developments and design. He disproved my wish to satisfy his need. He interrupted my rhythm to insert his rule and government. Personally, in looking back, I have found accommodation in the house of escape, God permits it but not without supervision and imposed limits regulated by frustrations and feelings of stagnation. **God knows all outcomes so he can manipulate the means to accomplish his intentions.** In so many of my efforts to succeed I have been stung by failures and tranquilized by repeated disappointments. God held failure in custody until success became illegal. God in his mercy and grace waited until my humility was in place then gave me victory predicated upon his loving kindness. In my attempt to succeed without him I was trying to escape him until failure became my portion and promise.

214

We Cannot Escape God

One of our greatest fights is running away from God. Running from God will not delay the chase or silence the caller. Running only means you have not come to terms with the conditions for submission and agreement. We cannot escape God even while we are in flight, his vigilance is supervising our escape. When we try to escape God he conditions the journey and cancels our options until his appointed time.

215

There are so many people in church trying to escape God. Some people are even in school trying to escape learning and class assignments. Some are in relationships trying to escape communication, on the job but trying to escape work. So many of us want life but we fight constantly to escape the principle elements that make life what it is. There are people who live on the run they are always in flight conditioned by the philosophy of escapism. *Escape is denial on the run and reality in retreat*

Are You Worthy Of Him?

This is the addiction in some cities of America where lives are riddled with one form of escapism or another. This is one of the reasons why America cannot resolve her issues with racism we will discuss superficially the phantoms of racism while escaping the core elements that determine the pathology. Jonah like so many in their dark thinking in America desires to kill what they fear and hate the most. Jonah wanted God to judge and destroy what he disliked not realizing what he disliked had everything to do with the contents and condition of his heart. His dislike was his disguise and distortion, his dislike disrobed his disposition regarding the temperament of God towards the Assyrians. Please be cautious with your dislikes make sure it does not incriminate your heart.

Please observe the psychology of Jonah's call he was sent to a wicked people who were more ready to accept change than the preacher who was assigned to bring change. Israel who refused to repent through the preaching of many prophets was shamed by the penitent posture of the wicked Assyrians who can be classified as the Isis of their day they were wicked, cruel and dominant yet they repented. They held the resolve to Jonah's heart condition yet he remained impenitent. God gives

Jonah the answer to his issues in his assignment to the Assyrians.

There were Jewish Kings like Jehoiakim who refuse to repent when warned by Jeremiah the prophet. Many of the Jews refuse to repent at the preaching of Jesus. Nineveh was willing with urgency to submit to the preaching of a stranger without questioning his authority or authenticity.

This lets us know that God is loving and compassionate towards those who are your enemies and he's willing to forgive them if they will repent. Nineveh was willing to change but Jonah was unwilling to change his heart towards them.

217

Escaping

It was the year 2004 that I heard this story from Pastor Jean Paul from Haiti, he told it in graphic detail as we spoke one Evening, highlighting the grace of God and the wonder of His love to those who pursue escaping his will. For almost 10 years the Lord had pleaded with Pastor Paul to return to Haiti to begin a work for him. He escaped by investing his time in his engineering career working his own business and busying himself with pursuing his own endeavors. He intentionally places the will of God on pause while investing in his own personal desires. When he left Haiti he was young and immature spiritually, but there was a prophetic word uttered over his life regarding his return to the land of his birth. The word of the Lord was specific and direct it was delivered to address his heart and the chosen intentions of God's will. "I will allow you to leave Haiti to attend bible school in the US, but you must return to your people after many years to fulfill my will for your life."

Pastor Paul heard and received these words in his youth as he prepared his heart to leave Haiti it was a time of excitement, opportunity, and adventure as he departed in his teenage years, on a music scholarship. After completing school both in music and engineering, life became prosperous and captivating, but the call of God was not. After many years of fine living, the will of God became stale, neglected and forgotten. One night after seasons of blessing and many warnings from the Lord, Pastor Paul had a dream.. In this dream his car was caught on a train track and the train was coming, but he could not move, then he heard the voice of the Lord, "if you don't return to Haiti this is what will happen to you."

Pastor Paul became so afraid after running from God for so long that he went to the bank the following morning, drew out all his money. He purchased a plane ticket and headed back to Haiti leaving his job, family and all of his accomplishments. In addition to this dream on the same night, he had the dream, his wife had the same dream and heard the terminating and menacing warning from the Lord. So his family was in total agreement that he had to run to do the will of God because his life was depended on it. Pastor Paul has four kids and a wife, but he had the call of God that propelled him beyond just the duties of family. As he left Atlanta, his journey in the prophetic will of God was initiated and there were many days of tears, trials, and testing. I am thankful today that we were able to give supportive aid to this call of God that furnish and facilitated the children and young adults of Haiti with salvation.

We cannot escape the call and prophetic desires of God for our life. Escape will only intensify the urgency of the call while deepening veracity of

219

his power and purpose. God will not be denied nor be deluded in his purposes. His purpose will stand and his word will be established. Escape may reduce your time by condensing the potency of your journey. Escape is the misuse of time, juxtapose with the confrontation of time maximized in pursuit of purpose. What we run from we tend to run into. **Escape is attempting to dismiss what persistently follows.** Escape is the absence of resolution and the presence of denial with an attitude. **We run when we lack the humility to surrender and the courage to obey. Running from God disables the runner because you are being chased by the one who owns your feet.**

220

Deliverance is in Your Enemies

God will use the change in your enemies to challenge the condition of your heart. Are you worthy of him if you are trying to escape your own deliverance? Jonah was reluctant because he was unforgiving towards the Assyrians. **The point is the work you are called to do is a mirror of the work God is doing in you.** It is safe to say that Nineveh was Jonah's therapeutic intervention a Cat-scan of his heart towards God. What we labor in, God works through to bring us to both healing and perfection.

This is so symptomatic of the conditions in America we so earnestly desire for our enemies to change yet we refuse to change ourselves. We refuse to see that some of our challenges are a mirror of what's unsolved in our own hearts. We desire to lead the world while our institutions and families are falling apart. We cannot ask the world to do what we are unwilling to resolve at home. We want to lead the world with a leadership vacuum in our homes and institutions regionally. We cannot escape home by policing the nations of the world.

What God did to Nineveh held the keys to Jonah's deliverance and healing. Jonah's heart towards Nineveh revealed his heart towards God. How you feel about your enemies is indicative of your thoughts toward God. **Unforgiveness is an attitude towards God that determines how we treat our enemies.** *How you treat your enemies will determine where you stumble or how you rise.* Our heart towards God allows us to see who the real enemy is and the place of influence that's given. Jonah was willing to use death as a way of escape rather than confront his need to change. His real enemy is exposed by what he was unwilling to do, this is suggestive of his heart towards God. When God was willing to show mercy he was requesting judgment in opposition to God. He was unwilling to change espousing a message of change. How can the reform of an unreformed reformer inspire reformation?

222

Failing to change is life escaping. Are you escaping in areas of your life where you refuse to change? ***Where change is absent escape is invoked in all its subtlety.*** So many in our churches and around the country are moving at rapid speed from marriage to marriage trying to escape in themselves what they hope to discover in the novelty of a new relationship. They keep running from themselves into themselves stumbling into what they refused to confront. ***Escape does not begin with our legs it is a condition of the heart.***

Our response to this unsaved world represents our escape from God. We escape when we resist witnessing by robbing people the opportunity to change. ***Where change is challenged escape anesthetizes the call.*** How can we deny others the very relationship that secures our redemptive custody? One of intrinsic features of working out your own salvation is sharing the Savior and Captain of your salvation. Notice that Christ came so that we might escape the consequences of sin. He did not come trying to escape the cross but provided for us a way of escape from the snares of death and hell. When we escape the Great Commission are we invalidating the God of our salvation? **How can we resist sharing what we have become through sharing?** Grace has been shared so that faith might be inescapable. What has been shared empowers us to share. **A shared life magnifies what's given through relationship and rewards.**

223

    We are escaping God at times unconsciously because we are blinded by the flight and distracted by false ambitions that compromise the Great Commission. Escaping God conveys a reality that is more disturbing than the flight. Escape is always attempting to step into a reality that is not governed or rule by God. The tools of our escape are renegade desires and rationalizations that feeds a darken conscience offsetting invitations to God's counsel. **Escape is the refuge of a rebellious heart. It is Christocentric betrayal besieged by hardness of heart.**

Are You Worthy Of Him?

In these seasons before the King of Kings return we must, unlike Jonah, foster in the hearts of many a place of repentance and surrender committing ourselves completely without reservation to the demands and commands of the Kingdom. Escape is not a healthy option because time holds us accountable and captive to his divine purposes. Eternity must be served to allow God to invade our world when God invades we tend to decide against what we know instinctively and beyond our frame of reference. The challenge for us is to run to God even when his will works against the grain and gravity of our desires. Running to him exposes the enemy giving us conquest that conditions our responses.

God made us for Himself and desires our time, love and devotion. We must persistently seek to cultivate and deepen our desire for him. In this season and the seasons ahead we need him even more desperately.

Are You Worthy of Him

Summary

To be worthy of God will cost you everything, it is initiated on the altar of complete surrender. It is only through surrender that the worth and dignity of his person can be known and seen in our lives. He must be loved more than anything you can ever know or imagine this is the worthiness of his person revealed to us. Our love for him purports a superlative degree that gives him the ultimate recognition of reality and relationship. Loving him is the authentication of life-giving validation to our worth. We must be willing to surrender all so that what remains is the inseparable oneness that confirms the prayer of Jesus in John 17:21.

Peter, James, and John were willing to forsake all in Luke 5:11 after Peter's obedience at the

225

lake Gennesaret brought him abundant blessings. God use abundance to bring conviction, confession, and commitment among his inner circle.

They saw the worth in following him when they embrace and experience the manifestation of his word. At the most lucrative day of their business, they were willing to forsake all to follow the worthiness of the King. They were willing to place relationship before resources, affection before abundance and supplier before distribution. The disciples allowed the most productive experience to become their most decisive hour. What God demonstrates can overwhelm you but who God is must humble you. Peter fell at the knees of Jesus and confess 'Lord depart from me I am a sinful man.'

The Lord cannot be compared or superseded by anything or anyone in our love engagement with him he is first and foundational. We must decide this or violate all our freedoms. When we decide that he is first we are not so much putting him first but agreeing that he is first dissolving if not inhibiting our own deceptions. We are worthy to the extent that we obey him in assurance with the manifestation of his word.

Our life must prove his life because we live

226

Summary

for him, not ourselves. Being worthy is premised upon what Christ has done not what we fail to imitate. Worthiness cannot be hijacked on an egotistical appraisal devoid of a centralized image of the cross. We are worthy as we look to him and look like him in all our character development. We are worthy of him as we honor him with our lives and conform to him through obedience to his word. We are not a worthy because of what we wear, where we live or what we drive. Worthiness must be dramatize and demonstrated by our capacity to change lives and impact communities and regions around the world. Worthiness is my annex to power that infiltrate homes, schools, institutions and systems of power. The worthiness of a King is in his regal capacity to take dominion and established a bastion of power.

It is our worthiness of him that serves as a great witness to the world. Failing to witness intentionally is refusing to reciprocate an opportunity that made us who we are. Our worthiness confirms the values of heaven and the authenticity of our love for God. The way we treat the unsaved displays our love for God because he died for them. How we decide to treat the unsaved is an index of our salvatory condition. Our love for God must be seen and experienced by the way we treat people

227

regardless of who they are and where they came from. This is the worthiness of our faith as it is portrayed in the very character of our walk? **We walk by faith to magnify the glory of his worthiness.**

When you are lost

you are lost

to your true worth

that's revealed

and established

in Christ.

Are You Worthy of Him?

Conclusion

We that are called the redeemed are both challenged and empowered by God to be all that he has called us to be. We must be bold and compelling, filled with the Holy Spirit willing to endure hardness as good soldiers of the Lord Jesus Christ. We must walk worthy as we believe if we disbelieve we tell lies about God and deny our destiny and worthiness in him. The most critical issue in this hour is the worthiness of our individual and collective walk. We are the solution to the world as we live worthy of him but in the absence of worthiness the world must be protected from us.

If we are not worthy individually we are not glorious or rapture ready collectively. The brightness of his glory must be seen more conspicuously as it darkens in the world. If we are not drawing people to him are we walking worthy of him? Christ is still the hunger and the unconscious desire of so many. What's unknown to so many of us is how necessary Christ is to life and life even more abundantly. A worthy walk punctuates the need and fulfills the desire to be what he has design and determined in us before the foundation of the world.

As we walk worthy of him the Father is well pleased because Jesus is the delight and revelation of the Father. When we are deserving of him in our walk it attracts the Father. The central purpose of our worthiness in Christ is to reveal the glory of the Father. We are made in his image and likeness to live deserving of him in every facet of our lives. A worthy lifestyle is the heritage of the redeemed and reconciled sons of God.

230

The central and cardinal reality of this book is to produce in us what we must confront and conform to as we behold him, we may be shaped by what we hear but we can only reproduce what we see. Jesus affirmed constantly that he only did what he saw the Father doing. Who-ever your father is you will always reproduce him because your eyes are attached to him. *A worthy walk is in the eye of your beholder.* We must choose today, *Christ saw your worth and died, can you see His worth and*

Conclusion

live for him. Walk worthy because his death is worthy and his life is deserving of all your sacrifices. The Spirit of the Lord is calling you to walk worthy of the one that empowered you to imitate his holy worthiness. Your worth is in him to walk unworthy is to betray the dignity of your value. Walk worthy of Him we are in the final hours there is no time for a pause or delay we must embrace the fierce exigencies of now.

This is the hour and season to seek God with profound intensity. 'Are you worthy of him' is a call, a challenge, and a conviction to live empowered by the Spirit of the living God. There is a constant and vigorous need for the church all over the world and particularly in America to pray as we transition into a time of impending danger and uncertainty for the world. The heart of the Father is still souls this is the reason why he sent his Son so that we might become an offspring of his heart pulsating the gravity of his intention and motivations.

231

This is a bright and meaningful time for great witnessing among the lost as we near the coming of Christ. Our worthiness should be more evident as the days draw closer to the coming of the King of Kings. The King is coming for a people called out in worthiness, holiness, and glory. **Walk worthy of him.**

Are You Worthy Of Him?

Walk worthy of him.

Walk worthy,
it ascribes honor
where
His glory
is absent.

232

Are You Worthy of Him?

Maxims

Maxims are rubies gleaned from the diadem of the heart.

Worthiness is the relational result of a centralized love objective.

The true value of my life is seen as it is surrendered not kept.

We cannot be seated in heaven yet live unworthy and undignified on the earth.

Are You Worthy Of Him?

We deserved him when we are empowered to experience what he lived by example.

A worthy walk means that the strength of your message must be balanced by the dignity of your character.

Greatness is processed in the laboratory of obedience.

The love of God cannot be received minus the nature of its impact.

234

So many of us have allowed the benefits of obedience, draw us away from the very purpose of obedience.

You cannot love God by seeking greatness from a world that resists God.

The world is in love with those it seeks to destroy.

Children will abort what they hear by becoming pregnant with what they see.

We are shaped by the callings of God before we respond to its obligations.

Your call is not just about you it's about the one who called you.

Maxims

Your call is not from God if it's not building character in God.

When obedience inspires death to self, life begins.

The reality of God is the practice of obedience.

Obedience is to the future what repentance is to the past. In the absence of obedience, you don't have a future.

Decisions are the resting place for your thoughts.

It's through the doors of thought you enter the house of decision.

Decision is the face of disposition.

You must bear the fruit of your choices in order to confront the face of your character.

A mind design for glory is a condition by the end of a thing.

To obey you must come to terms with the conditions for following.

There are many who follow Jesus but not for Jesus.

Pride is strength in areas where God is absent it's the

235

strength of your weaknesses.

We are not freed by our definition of the truth but by its revelation of us

When your needs become Lord you prostitute identity.

There's no test you can take in God that Jesus did not pass.

Failing to change is life escaping. Where change is absent escape is present.

Your love for God can fall while your work is still standing.

There are some things you have to forget to stay clean and there are other things you must remember to remain pure.

Christ saw your worth and died for you, can you see His worth and live for him.

Unforgiveness is an attitude towards God that determines how we treat our enemies.

The work you are called to do is a mirror of the work

God is doing in you.

God is inescapable even while we are in flight his omniscience is supervising our escape.

A worthy walk ascribes value where his glory is absent.

Who you are matters to God because it is measured by his life.

Obedience is the most natural response to who we love.

A shared life magnifies what's given through relationship and reward.

Escape does not begin with our legs it's a condition of the heart.

Preparation is the face of purpose and the character of process.

Preparation is purpose in storage and potential on pause.

Escape is denial on the run and reality in retreat.

Escape is attempting to dismiss what persistently follows.

How you treat your enemies will determine why you

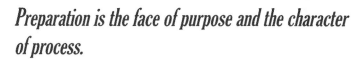

stumble or how you rise.

A nation is defined by what parents are doing.

Parenting is the industry of the family that determines the business of kids.

The cattle is only as healthy as the pasture in which it was raised.

The impact of Christ on the world is conditioned and concentrated in the activities of his Father.

When we die to self we have a weapon when we resist death Satan is weaponized.

Fabian F. Harper
Biography

Fabian F. Harper has faithfully served in ministry for over 30 years in a variety of callings and capacities. He is a tremendously gifted and inspirational speaker with a seasoned and revelatory approach to the teaching of God's word. He is a wise counselor and dedicated mentor to many youths and young adults. He is also an insightful and compelling author of several thought engaging books, booklets, and instructive manuals.

Fabian has worked extensively as a Counselor with adults and even more so with the adolescent population in a variety of facilities throughout Georgia, he has also worked as a Pastoral Counselor, Family Counselor, Pastor, Associate Pastor, Executive Pastor, Director Of Missions, Decorator, Mentor and founder of The Reform Society & Kingdom Allegiance Ministries. Fabian has been married for over thirty years to Patrice N. Harper and is the father of one daughter and two grand-daughters that now resides in Atlanta Georgia. He is a conference speaker that brings light, passion and profound revelation to congregation wherever he goes. He's available for revivals, workshops and instructive teachings that advance the Kingdom of God. Fabian holds four University degrees and now Pastor's 'Kingdom Allegiance Ministries' in Atlanta Georgia.

240

Fabian F. Harper

Making The Kingdom Of Christ Known Throughout All Humanity.

Other Books, Booklets And Instructive Manuals By Fabian F. Harper

Stepping Out Of Your Boat

We stand today at gunpoint with the bullets of restraint aimed at our unlimited potential found in Christ. Stepping Out Of Your Boat is design to lift us above the challenges that are mundane into the dimension of the impossible.

242

Stepping Out Of Your Boat

Revised Edition

It is time to dress ourselves in the garments
of the impossible through progressive steps
of faith.

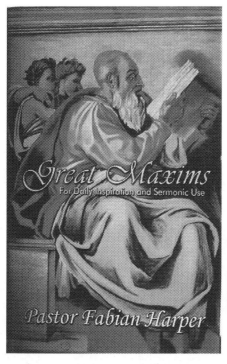

Great Maxims

For Daily Inspiration And Sermonic Use

First Edition

The entrance to Godly wisdom is never closed.
Great Maxims are rubies of treasure gleaned from
the diadem of the heart. It is the cream that gives
credibility to the King's thoughts.

Great Maxims

For Daily Inspiration And Sermonic Use

Second Edition

It is by wisdom Kings reign in majesty while citizens decree what is just, righteous and noble in the earth. Wisdom is greater than strength more valuable than weapons of war.

To Live is To Love:

We must love be-
yond what we
know to live be-
yond what we see
and conceptualize.

245

Love Activates Faith

Our confidence in
God is the strength
of our love for God.
We love on the
level of our faith.

Opportunity is Chance

Purpose is optimized through opposition and opportunity. Opposition is the friend of purpose and the servant of opportunity.

246

Intimacy The Fullness of Identity

It is the source of creation that announces the worth and identity of the created.

247

Watch What You Practice:

It is the practices of the heart that impassions the journey of the soul.

Notes

Notes

Notes

Printed in the United States
By Bookmasters